MATHEMATICS AND THE
IMAGE OF REASON

PHILOSOPHICAL ISSUES IN SCIENCE
General Editor
W. H. Newton-Smith

MATHEMATICS AND THE IMAGE OF REASON

Mary Tiles

London and New York

First published 1991
by Routledge
11 New Fetter Lane, London EC4P 4EE

Simultaneously published in the USA and Canada
by Routledge
a division of Routledge, Chapman and Hall, Inc.
29 West 35th Street, New York, NY 10001

Typeset in 10/12 Times by
J&L Composition Ltd, Filey, North Yorkshire
Printed and bound in Great Britain by
TJ Press (Padstow) Ltd, Padstow, Cornwall

British Library Cataloguing in Publication Data
Tiles, Mary
Mathematics and the image of reason.
1. Mathematics. Philosophical perspectives, history
I. Title   II. Series
510.1

Library of Congress Cataloging in Publication Data
Tiles, Mary.
Mathematics and the image of reason / Mary Tiles.
p.   cm. — (Philosophical issues in science)
Includes bibliographical references (p.)
1. Mathematics—Philosophy.   2. Frege, Gottlob, 1848–1925.
3. Russell, Bertrand, 1872–1970.   4. Hilbert, David, 1862–1943.
I. Title.   II. Series.
QA8.4.T538   1991
510'.1—dc20   90–8971

ISBN 0–415–03318–7

TO ALAN

For, Things Mathematical, being (in a manner) middle between the supernatural and the natural, are not so absolute and excellent as things supernatural, nor yet so base and gross as things natural, but are things immaterial, and nevertheless, by things material able somewhat to be signified. And though their particular images, by Art, are aggregable and divisible, yet the general Forms not withstanding, are constant, unchangeable, untransformable, and incorruptible. Neither of sense can they, at any time, be perceived or judged. Nor yet, for all that, in the royal mind of man first conceived. But surmounting the imperfection of conjecture, weening and opinion, and coming short of high intellectual conception, are the Mercurial fruit of Dialectical discourse, in perfect imagination subsisting. A marvellous neutrality have these things Mathematical, and also a strange participation between things supernatural, immortal, simple and indivisible, and things natural, mortal, sensible, compounded and divisible. Probability and sensible proof may well serve in things natural, and is commendable. In mathematical reasonings, a probable argument is nothing regarded, nor yet the testimony of the sense any whit credited, but only a perfect demonstration of truths, certain, necessary and invincible, universally and necessarily concluded is allowed sufficient for an argument exactly and purely mathematical.

John Dee (1570)

CONTENTS

CONTENTS

ACKNOWLEDGEMENTS

I wish to thank Bill Newton-Smith for encouraging and facilitating the production of this book, Ray Mines for discussion, for bringing relevant material to my attention and for reassurance that there are mathematicians willing to talk about the philosophy of mathematics. Thanks also to Jim for having lived with the whole writing process.

INTRODUCTION

Post-modernists proclaim the failure of the projects of the Enlightenment – the death of philosophy, epistemology, morality, imagination and reason. Nietzsche announced the death of God and with him died all hope of founding either a secular morality or a secular epistemology. If God is dead, then so too is 'that of God in every man', that 'natural light of reason' by which the Good and the True stand revealed. Even mathematics suffers a loss of certainty (Kline 1980). Yet in the very culture within which this loss occurs there has a arisen a new faith – the cult of information technology, of the computer, of scientific facts and figures. But how can numerical representation and computation be worshipped in this way after the death of the mathematician-god, architect of the universe, and after the discrediting of the myth of a super-sensible mathematical reality? Because, as in all supplanting of one faith by another, there is a supporting mythology of conquering and vanquished heroes. Transcendent reason, on which the Enlightenment pinned its hopes, has been imprisoned in formal, computational chains and it is the celebration of this victory which forms a necessary, legitimating complement to post-modernist claims. Enlightenment is impossible because reason has been rendered practically and theoretically impotent; it is confined to symbol manipulation, infallibly tracing paths through symbol structures, but incapable of showing a way out of these man-made 'information'-labyrinths, or even of determining the transition from one such labyrinth to another.

A striking feature of mathematics is that it has two distinct faces – its number-crunching, calculatory face, revealed in applications, and its almost number- and calculation-free face, revealed in the pure mathematicians' study of abstract structures. Somehow

1

these are related; somehow the non-wordly, abstract study where theorems are proved with an exactness and certitude unparalleled in other branches of knowledge yields powerful methods and techniques for dealing with the physical world. Reason delivers, with apparent certainty, knowledge of an abstract, non-empirical realm, knowledge which is nonetheless of immense practical utility in the empirical world. Is it then any wonder that this should be treated as the paradigmatic manifestation of the *power* of reason? But at the same time this very power presents a puzzle and a philosophical challenge – how is it possible?

The mystery can be temporarily dispelled by the postulation of a mathematician-god, creator and architect of both the universe and the mind of man, or simply of the minds of all men, determining the forms of their experience and of their thought and ensuring the possibility of a concordance between the two. The pure mathematicians' mathematics, which has led to Pythagoreanism, Platonism and number mysticism, yields an image of a pure contemplative reason with the power to transcend the empirical world, to glimpse the Reality beyond, to participate in the Creator's ideas, learning to read the language of His universe and/or the super-sensible realm of Forms. This solution does, however, leave transcendent, mathematical reason hostage to the fate of God or of our ability to participate in His knowledge. If God is dead, or if we may not presume to share His knowledge, then the transcending power of mathematical reason also vanishes, stripped of its credentials as a source of knowledge. Mathematics is then reduced to its applications; it is a source only of convenient representational and calculatory devices. The number crunching involved in applied mathematics, which predominates in technological thinking, spawns a calculatory image of reason.

Perhaps the power of reason was mischaracterized and the philosophical problem misposed. The failure of one solution to the puzzle of the two faces of mathematics does not necessarily entail the failure of all solutions. The way in which the puzzle is made precise, the exact formulation of the philosophical problem posed, is as open to question as its metaphysical solution. It remains the case, however, that any account of mathematics must address itself to the characterization and the relation of the two aspects of mathematics, resisting either a reduction to a single aspect or a mystificatory unification via a metaphysical postulation.

Mathematics has been heavily implicated in both the formation of Enlightenment aspirations and the subsequent (post-modern) imprisonment of reason, for it is mathematics which, from Plato and Aristotle onward, has been the locus of images of reason in western culture. Mathematics is the paradigmatically rational discipline, sometimes serving as the source of images of reason, at other times subject to constraint by images derived from other sources. It is by focussing on mathematics that the story of the capture of reason within formal, computational chains is revealed to be a myth, albeit one with an origin in logicist and formalist programmes for the foundations of mathematics, which were formulated toward the end of the nineteenth century and were dedicated to the abolition of reliance on intuition in mathematics. Had these programmes been successfully completed, mathematical reason would have been shown to be confinable within formal, computational bounds via the erection of structures of confinement. But these programmes were not successfully completed; they were decisively demonstrated not to be completable as originally proposed – a rare event indeed in philosophical history.

The chains for reason were forged by mathematicians of the late nineteenth and early twentieth century as they attempted to secure the foundations of analysis and to banish reliance on intuition. Formal systems and computational methods were developed in pursuit of the logicist and formalist programmes for the foundations of mathematics. When it is acknowledged that these programmes failed, the lessons drawn from their failure depend crucially on how the programmes themselves are characterized. If their goal was to put mathematics on logically secure foundations, then a demonstration that this cannot be done may be perceived as leaving the way open to scepticism about mathematics, to a loss of certainty. Alternatively, however, one might be prompted to question logicist and formalist conceptions of what constitutes a foundation, or one might question the whole idea that knowledge claims require legitimation in secure foundations. If the goal of logicist and formalist programmes was to vindicate empiricist claims that mathematics is devoid of content, that its language is a non-distorting medium of convenience in which theories of empirical science can safely be written without prejudice to their empirical objectivity, then their failure represents a significant setback to empiricist philosophies, and empiricist philosophies of science in particular (see Wang 1986). This interpretation contributed to the demise of the conceit that empirical science is founded on a bedrock of observations which are untainted by interpretation or prior conceptualization.

But even as this consequence was acknowledged (in the work of Quine, Popper, Feyerabend, Kuhn and others) the presumption remained that the logicist/formalist account of the nature of reason (here including mathematical reason) was correct: theoretical reason reduces to formal logic, which itself can be reduced to computational rules for manipulating symbols. When reason, so confined, proves unable to justify itself, it comes under attack; the rationality of science is put in question. Since the reasoning involved in science can readily be shown not to be confinable within formal, computational bounds, it can be shown not to be rational. Science stands unmasked; its authority does not lie in the rationality of its methods but in the politics of power relations. In so far as mathematics is continuous with empirical science its theories will be subject to the same indeterminacies, the same lack of rational constraint in their development; they will be subject only to loose empirical or sociological constraints (see Putnam 1975, Kitcher 1983, Maddy 1984 and Anellis 1989 for example). It is in this way that the computational image of reason serves as the legitimating complement to post-modern rejections of reason.

But why should that computational image be accepted? Can one not justifiably read the failure of the logicist and formalist programmes as revealing the inadequacies of this conception of reason? The burden of this book is to show that and how this is possible; it will be argued that mathematics is neither an exemplification of transcendent reason, nor mere calculation of logical consequences, but human knowledge of structures gained by employing reason beyond the bounds of logic. If this conception of mathematics can be sustained, mathematics could once again serve as a source of an image of reason liberated from formal imprisonment, freed to confront apocalyptic post-modern visions. If reason has not died in confinement but can escape, transfigured, the same may be true of philosophy, morality, epistemology, history and imagination.

My claim will be that the image of reason which needs to be resurrected in a suitably transfigured form (a form which involves a displacement of the transcendental deduction and of transcendental reasoning) is that which Kant developed in his account of mathematics and the synthetic *a priori*. There are three reasons for this: (i) of all the philosophers of the eighteenth century it was

4

Kant who saw with full clarity the highly problematic character of the project of developing a mathematical physics and who approached this problem in a wholly new way; (ii) Kant's account of the synthetic *a priori*, which is the core of his account of the power of theoretical reason and hence of mathematics, of experimental science and of philosophy, is ultimately grounded in his conception of the rational agent, an agent who is able to act not only according to a rule but also according to his conception of a rule, and who thereby is also a moral agent; (iii) Hilbert, whose work in so many ways influenced the course and character of twentieth-century mathematics, himself worked within a basically Kantian framework.

But, it will be objected, hasn't Kant's account of the synthetic character of mathematics been shown to be quite untenable (i) by the discovery of non-Euclidean geometry and (ii) by the intuitionist mathematicians who have shown that a Kantian approach to arithmetic would require the rejection of much of classical analysis? These objections will be considered in Chapter 5, where it will be argued that, whilst they do require a rejection of the details of Kant's account of arithmetic and geometry, they do not impinge on the core of his account of mathematical reason – the account of synthetic *a priori* knowledge as knowledge gained by employing reason beyond the bounds set by formal, logical rules. This is knowledge of structures generated by imposing or following rules, knowledge which is possible only for a being which is able to conceptualize rules and rule following in addition to being able to act in accordance with them.

The regulated activities of a being capable of reflective judgement concerning its own rule following do not form a closed system. The system is always finite, but always carries within it the potential for extension and for modification through extension; it is *potentially* infinite. But, unlike the potentially infinite series of the natural numbers, which, being generated by a single rule (repeated addition of a unit) admits of reflective totalization, the indefinite extensibility of the system of rules resists totalization because it is not itself rule governed. To affirm this is to do no more and no less than to affirm the possibility of creativity in mathematics and the freedom of development regulated by the *ideal* of total rational systematization. In the late twentieth century intuition is becoming mathematically respectable once more as mathematicians use computers to help them develop methods of studying nonlinear functions in ways which have never before been available to them (the theory of chaos). In a step which I would want to claim is typical of the life of reason, but which is most clearly illustrated in the history of mathematics, the effort to axiomatize, to rigorize, to secure foundations has itself made possible development in a wholly new direction; it has spawned a mathematics outside that which was being safely secured and systematized.

Regulation by an unattainable ideal is possible only for a being capable of reflective judgement and is to be distinguished from being rule governed. To characterize human rationality in terms of rule governed activity is either to reduce man to the level of a machine or to elevate him to the level of a perfect rational being, the attained ideal. It is precisely this oscillation that we find manifest in attitudes toward computers, the embodiments of rule governed, calculatory 'reason'; they are alternately mere machines and superior intellects. By focussing on the ways in which mathematicians of the late nineteenth and early twentieth centuries sought to rigorize and systematize mathematics we see a noncalculatory reason at work even as it seeks to impose a calculatory ideal. It is an example of reason deployed in pursuit of a rational ideal functioning regulatively. We also see the transforming power of this activity. It changed the face of mathematics, its scope, its methods and its self-image in ways which were unforeseen and unpredictable and this included the production of results, such as Gödel's theorem, which displaced the calculatory ideal itself by showing it to be unrealizable. There is, then, a price to be paid for freedom to deploy reason in the pursuit of ideals – a loss of predictability and an opening up to the possibility of a radical critique of the ideals of prediction control and efficiency projected by the mechnical, computational image of reason. But if the mechanical image *is* flawed, as the collapse of logicist and formalist programmes suggests, then it is as dangerous to attempt to live by its ideals as it is to abandon the ways of reason.

1

AXIOMATIZATION, RIGOUR AND REASON

After deserting for a time the old Euclidean standards of rigour, mathematics is now returning to them, and even making efforts to go beyond them.

(Frege 1950 p. 1e)

RIGOUR AND PROOF

A distinctive feature of mathematics, that feature in virtue of which it stands as a paradigmatically rational discipline, is that assertions are not accepted without proof. To establish, for example, that the internal angles of a triangle add up to two right angles, it is neither sufficient nor appropriate to go round measuring the internal angles of triangular figures. By proof is meant a deductively valid, rationally compelling argument which shows why this *must* be so, given what it is to be a triangle. But arguments always have premises so that if there are to be any proofs there must also be starting points, premises which are agreed to be necessarily true, self-evident, neither capable of, nor standing in need of, further justification. The conception of mathematics as a discipline in which proofs are required must therefore also be a conception of a discipline in which a systematic and hierarchical order is imposed on its various branches. Some propositions appear as first principles, accepted without proof, and others are ordered on the basis of how directly they can be proved from these first principles. Basic theorems, once proved, are then used to prove further results, and so on. Thus there is a sense in which, so long as mathematicians demand and provide proofs, they must necessarily organize their discipline along lines approximating to the pattern to be found in Euclid's *Elements*.

7

In what sense, then, could mathematics have deserted the old Euclidean standards of rigour, as Frege claimed? To understand Frege's complaint it is first necessary to note that the conception of a proof, or of the possibility of establishing propositions by rationally compelling means, is inherently problematic in that it apparently requires two distinct kinds of rational capacity – the ability to reason, to construct an argument which involves a number of steps each of which must be rationally compelling (discursive reason), and the ability to recognize first principles and to perceive the necessity of their truth (rational intuition). This apparent need to invoke two rational faculties can be illustrated in the case of Euclid's geometry. For example, consider Euclid's proposition 32, the geometrical proof which appears to have been Aristotle's favourite example (Euclid 1926 pp. 320–1).

In any triangle, if one of the sides be produced, the exterior angle is equal to the two interior and opposite angles, and the three interior angles of the triangle are equal to two right angles.

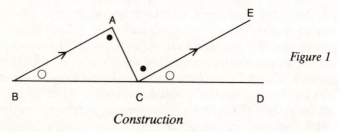

Figure 1

Construction

Let ABC be a triangle and let one side of it, BC, be produced to D (Postulate 2) and CE be drawn through the point C parallel to the straight line AB (I.31).

Proof

BAC = ACE – alternate angles between parallel lines are equal (I.29).

ECD = ABC – corresponding angles with parallel lines are equal (I.29).

Therefore ACD = ACE + ECD = BAC + ABC and
    BAC + ABC + ACB = ACD + ACB = 2 right angles (I.13)

Q.E.D.

Here there is a process of reasoning employing the following.

1 Wholly general principles such as that if $a = c$ and $b = d$, then $a + b = c + d$. These are listed by Euclid as Common Notions, or Axioms.
2 Results previously established, but which, if challenged, could also be proved (given here by numerical reference – I.13 is proposition 13 of Euclid Book I).
3 Principles peculiar to geometry for which no proof can be given, such as:

   All right angles are equal to one another (Euclid's postulate 4).

   A finite straight line can be produced continuously in a straight line (Euclid's postulate 2).
4 Definitions of triangle, right angle, parallel line etc.

If the result about triangles is to be regarded as proved, established beyond question, then not only must the steps in the argument be accepted as rationally compelling, but the principles of geometry to which appeal is made must be known to be true and thought to be such that, even though they have no proof, no rational person could call them into question. Further, the definitions to which appeal is made must be understood and judged to be correct, or appropriate; they must be agreed to capture what is essential about triangles etc. This was not conceived to be just a matter of providing a verbal definition; it had to be a definition which can serve as a starting point for demonstrations of the properties of triangles. The essence, the account of what-it-is-to-be a triangle, is that from which all other properties of the triangle flow. The achievement of an account of essence is thus itself the acquisition of knowledge about triangles.

It was for these reasons that Aristotle saw wisdom (*sophia*) as requiring two component abilities: the ability to give explanations and justifications (*episteme*), and a developed intuitive ability to recognize first principles (*nous*), which includes the ability to understand and see the correctness of accounts of essence. The function of a proof of a proposition is then to give an explanation of *why* it *must* be true. It is presumed that it may very well be known *that* the proposition in question is true before proof is provided. Thus, for both Aristotle and Euclid, the process of discovery is separated from the process of proof. The proof of a proposition gives no indication of how its truth was discovered. In his *Prior and Posterior Analytics*, Aristotle laid down the formal, logical standards which any proof would be required to meet. A proof should take the form of a valid syllogism or sequence of syllogisms. So, for example, we might argue as follows:

> All triangles are plane figures bounded by three straight lines.
> All plane figures bounded by three straight lines contain three angles.
> Therefore, all triangles contain three angles.

This would be a valid (first figure) syllogism which connects being a triangle to containing three angles via the property of being bounded by three straight lines (the middle term of the syllogism). We might further request proof of the second premisse, i.e. we might ask for the connection between being bounded by three straight lines and containing three angles. Our proof would then start to turn into a sequence of syllogisms the construction of which would require us to find a chain of middle terms which would link being a triangle with containing three angles. (For a more detailed account of syllogistic logic see Kneale and Kneale 1962). This emphasis on formal procedures of proof gives the impression of privileging the reasoning process (discursive reason) as the vehicle of, and route to, rational knowledge, understanding. Intuition, although clearly necessary, receives scant attention in this text, which was destined to form the basis of orthodox scholastic teaching on these matters. Thus the standards of rigour which dominated the image of reason within scholastic philosophy were those associated with deductive logic, in particular as concerned with the formal theory of syllogistic argument.

DESERTING EUCLIDEAN STANDARDS

The desertion of scholastic conceptions of Euclidean rigour can be fairly precisely identified with the rise of the so-called 'way of ideas', i.e. with the sixteenth- and seventeenth-century rejection of Aristotelian Scholasticism, the revival of interest in mathematics, the resurrection and elevation of the works of Archimedes by Galileo and others, and the rapid development of algebraic methods. The conception of reason associated with this movement is one which explicitly took the mathematical employment of reason as its ideal, and it is most clearly spelt out by Descartes.

To illustrate the kind of departure from Euclidean standards of rigour which this approach licensed it is helpful to consider the character of Archimedes' mathematical work since this was much admired by both Descartes and Galileo. It is significant, however, that they did not have available to them Archimedes' short treatise on method, which was only discovered by Heiberg in 1906. In this treatise Archimedes explains the methods which he used to find the areas and volumes of geometric figures and solids and distinguishes clearly in these methods between methods which were sufficient to suggest the truth of the propositions he wished to assert and the rigorous, strictly geometrical methods which would be required to prove these propositions. He says:

> First then I will set out the very first theorem which became known to me by means of mechanics, namely that
> *Any segment of a right angled cone (i.e. a parabola) is four-thirds of the triangle which has the same base and equal height,*
> and after this I will give each of the other theorems investigated by the same method. Then, at the end of the book, I will give the geometrical [proofs of the propositions] ...
> (Archimedes 1912 p. 14)

The method of discovery which Archimedes employed involved using an analogy from statics.

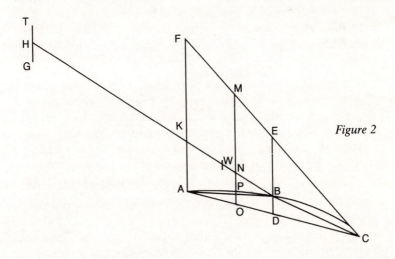

Figure 2

His idea was to try to 'balance' the triangle AFC (whose area and centre of gravity W can be calculated and whose area can be proved to be four times that of the triangle ABC) against the corresponding segment of the parabola by piling up all the line segments, such as OP, making up the parabola at a single point H (TG = OP). The theory of the balance then gives the ratio between the area of the triangle and that of the segments of the parabola. Archimedes argues that there will be equilibrium when HK = 3KW, so the area of the segment ABC must be a third of that of triangle AFC and hence four-thirds of the area of triangle ABC.

Archimedes sets out the argument more fully than has been done here. He lists his assumptions and conducts his arguments exactly as if he were constructing a geometrical proof. Why, then, does he not consider it to be a proof? This is because it involves importing conceptions from statics and the theory of levers, conceptions which do not belong to geometry at all. To give a *geometric* proof the starting points must be geometric assumptions and the concepts used must be geometric concepts. A similar consideration arises in relation to Archimedes' treatment of spirals and of the conic sections (parabola, ellipse, hyperbola). These were classed as mechanical curves because, although it was possible to define them via devices for constructing them, they could not be defined in terms of ruler and compass construction alone, i.e. in terms of circles and straight lines which are Euclid's primitives. Archimedes' definition of the spiral has to use a combination of linear and circular *motion*, rather than lines and circles.

> If a straight line drawn in a plane revolve at a uniform rate about one extremity which remains fixed and return to the position from which it started, and if, at the same time as the line revolves, a point move at a uniform rate along the straight line beginning from the extremity which remains fixed, the point will describe a **spiral** in the plane.
>
> (Archimedes 1897 p. 165)

This is the definition on the basis of which theorems about spirals are proved and the proofs have to make essential use of some simple propositions about uniform motion. In the Scholastic/Euclidean tradition the theory of these curves was therefore not regarded as being strictly geometrical.

Descartes, although an admirer of Archimedes, was not aware of his methodological sensitivity to and awareness of the stringent requirements of Euclidean rigour. Descartes professes not to be able to make any sense of the distinction between mechanical and geometrical curves. Instead he proposes

> if we make the usual assumption that geometry is precise and exact, while mechanics is not; and if we think of geometry as the science which furnishes a general knowledge of the measurement of all bodies, then we have no more right to exclude the more complex curves than the simpler ones, provided they can be conceived of as described by a continuous motion or by several successive motions, each motion being completely determined by those which precede; for in this way an exact knowledge of the magnitude of each is always obtainable.
>
> (Descartes 1925 p. 43)

In other words, Descartes is prepared to include motion as a simple geometrical concept (although he does not admit the complex of motions required to generate the spiral). It is something of which he has a clear and distinct idea, one which is suitable for inclusion in geometrical definitions. Axioms concerning motion (such as the conservation of momentum) will likewise be considered to have the same self-evident character as geometrical axioms. Archimedes' mechanical methods seem to Descartes to meet all the standards required for rigour and exactness. This means that by equating volume with quantity of matter (something which Archimedes does but only as part of a heuristic device) Descartes effectively blurs the distinction between geometry and mechanics. Here we have one clear departure from Euclidean standards of rigour which insists on sharp disciplinary boundary lines, but it was a departure which was crucial to the early development of mathematical physics. Rational mechanics could be pursued as an *a priori* discipline, one in which the methods of infinitesimal calculus could be developed by reliance on intuitions about continuous, uniform and uniformly accelerated motions, using these intuitions to avoid the absurdities that might otherwise result from calculating with 'vanishing' or 'infinitely small' magnitudes.

In addition Descartes rejects the syllogistically circumscribed conception of reasoning because he is in search of, and indeed imagines that he has found, a method of discovery, not merely of proof. The method of discovery is integral to his introduction of algebraic methods into geometry, which in turn leads him to urge the case for very significant departures from Euclid. The method is that of analysis–synthesis, something which is discussed by Euclid in Book XIII of his *Elements*, but for which the best surviving ancient source is Pappus (who is mentioned by Descartes).

> Analysis then takes that which is sought as if it were admitted and passes from it through successive consequences to something which is admitted as the result of synthesis: for in analysis we assume that which is sought as if it were (already) done, and we inquire what it is from which this results, and again what is the antecedent cause of the latter and so on, until, by so retracing our steps we come upon something already known or belonging to the class of first principles, and such a method we call analysis as being solution backwards.
>
> But in synthesis, reversing the process, we take as already done that which was last arrived at in the analysis and, by arranging in their natural order as consequences what were before antecedents, and successively connecting them one with another, we arrive finally at the construction which was sought, and this we call synthesis.
>
> (Editor's note in Euclid 1926: vol. I pp. 138–9)

In analysis, then, one reasons backwards from the proposition to be proved, by assuming it to be true and then looking for those simpler propositions which would have to be true in order to make it true (this being conceived as reasoning from effect to cause). The process stops when either one reaches first principles or previously proved theorems, or one reaches a proposition known to be false. In the latter case one concludes that the original proposition cannot, after all, be true. In the former, a proof of the original proposition is then sought by reversing the steps of the analysis (reasoning now from cause to effect). Descartes describes his use of algebra to solve geometric problems in precisely similar terms.

> If, then, we wish to solve any problem, we first suppose that solution already effected and give names to all the lines that seem needful for its construction – to those which are

unknown as well as to those that are known. Then, making no distinction between known and unknown lines, we must unravel the difficulty in any way that shows most naturally the relations between these lines, until we find it possible to express a single quantity in two ways. This will constitute an equation ... we must find as many such equations as there are supposed to be unknown lines.

(Descartes 1925 pp. 6–7)

Letters x, y etc. are introduced to stand for unknown magnitudes, which are nonetheless treated in exactly the same way as those which are known, i.e. one calculates with the letters, algebraically, just as if they were fixed and known magnitudes. By relating known magnitudes to unknown magnitudes in sets of simultaneous equations one can then solve for the unknowns.

It is clear that Descartes has moved a long way from what Pappus had in mind. However, since the detailed analysis of the character of Cartesian analysis is not our present concern, it is sufficient to note the self-conscious imitation of Pappus in Descartes' presentation of his use of algebra in geometry. We thus see that the analytic methods associated by Descartes with the use of algebraic techniques in geometry form the basis of his claim to have a method of discovery and provide his model for the use of reason as an instrument of discovery, and not merely of justification, in areas outside geometry. The consequences of this reorientation are more explicitly set out in Arnauld's influential work *The Port-Royal Logic*, where Euclidean standards of rigour are criticized in some detail. The Cartesian conception of reason, which underlies not only *The Port-Royal Logic* but also the works of Locke, Berkeley and Hume, is in many respects the polar opposite of that associated with mathematics in the wake of the work of Frege, Russell and Hilbert, work which Russell saw as reinstating an essentially scholastic view of the nature of mathematics.

What we find is that the priority of the two types of rational faculty is reversed. Instead of limiting reason to discursive reasoning, exhibited in the construction of formally valid arguments, Descartes reduces discursive reasoning to a sequence of intuitions. Reason is basically an *intuitive* faculty.

Hence we distinguish this mental intuition from deduction by the fact that into the conception of the latter there enters a

15

certain movement or succession, into that of the former there does not.

(Descartes 1931: rule III p. 8)

all knowledge whatsoever, other than that which consists in the simple and naked intuition of single independent objects, is a matter of the comparison of two things or more with each other. In fact practically the whole of the task set the human reason consists in preparing for this operation; for when it is open and simple we need no aid from art, but are bound to rely on the light of nature alone, in beholding the truth which comparison gives us.

(Descartes 1931: rule XIV p. 55)

Method, the analysis of problems and the systematic organization of their solutions is a necessary prerequisite for the employment of this intuitive faculty when it is finite, limited and imperfect, as it is in human minds. The same intuitive faculty when possessed by God, an infinite and perfect being, has no need to go through discursive reasoning processes in order to achieve its intuitive knowledge. In finite human minds, then, the use of reason is dependent upon possession of an ability to analyse, organize and structure, an ability which is essentially practical and strategic (as emphasized by the full title of *The Port-Royal Logic – la logique ou l'art de penser*). All reasoning, in the production of proofs and arguments, becomes a linking in the mind, a forming into a single intuition of a sequence of individual connections each of which is intuitively recognized to be correct.

From this point of view, something close to an axiomatic method is still central to the conception of correct mathematical procedure, but the emphasis on intuition points to a reorientation of the employment of this method, a reorientation which entails an alteration in what will constitute a proof and in what sorts of propositions may be taken as first principles. The hierarchical ordering is now required by, and is thus grounded in, the structure of the human mind as it works toward integrated intuitions; it is not an order objectively required by (intuitive) reason for to this reason all truths are equally immediate and evident.

What is agreed is that the proper ordering of a discipline requires that record should be made of:

16

1 any simple, undefined terms;
2 other terms to be used, supplied with definitions which use only the undefined terms already introduced;
3 general principles applicable to any subject matter;
4 principles containing the listed terms which are taken to be true without proof.

Arnauld's criticisms of the way in which geometers, including Euclid, have proceeded are the following:

(a) paying more attention to certitude than to evidentness and to convincing the mind than enlightening it;
(b) proving things that do not require proof;
(c) using demonstration by *reductio ad absurdum*;
(d) using roundabout demonstrations;
(e) ignoring the natural order.

These are interrelated complaints, centred on (e) which Arnauld explains as follows:

> Ignoring the natural order of knowledge is the geometer's greatest defect. He fancies that the only order he is called upon to observe is the order which makes the earlier propositions usable in demonstrating later ones. The geometers treat pell-mell of lines and surfaces and triangles and squares, proving by complicated figures the properties of simple lines and introducing numerous inversions which mar a beautiful science. Such procedures disregard the rules of true method, which tell us always to begin with the most simple and most general things, in order to pass on to those which are more complicated and more specific.
>
> (Arnauld 1964 p. 330)

The crucial concept here is that of 'natural order'. The point of axiomatization and the provision of proofs either directly from axioms or by reference to previously proved theorems is that a rational order is imposed. But what makes one order rather than another a rational order? Arnauld's demand is that the order imposed should reflect the way in which we come to learn and understand things, for knowledge is not simply a matter of having true beliefs but of understanding why something is the case. The order is to be the natural order of human thought, the order by which the mind will be led to an intuitive understanding.

The place to start (the undefined terms and axioms) is determined by what can be immediately understood and recognized to be true (clearly and distinctly perceived) and which thus stands in no need of proof. It will only confuse matters and misrepresent the order of knowledge if we try to prove that which is already known without proof. Thus Euclid is criticized for proving that the sum of the lengths of any two sides of a triangle is greater than the length of the third side. This, says Arnauld, is already evident from the very notion of a straight line, which 'is the shortest distance between two points and is a natural measure of the distance from one point to another'. Arnauld goes on to locate the source of Euclid's tendency to provide these unnecessary proofs:

> Euclid's insistence on proving the evident is doubtless a result of his failure to realise that all certainty and evidentness of our knowledge in the natural sciences springs from this principle: We can affirm of the idea of a thing everything which is contained in the clear and distinct idea of that thing.
>
> (Arnauld 1964 p. 330)

This is the cornerstone of the conception of rational knowledge enshrined in the way of ideas. Even though empiricists, such as Locke and Hume, rejected rationalist accounts of what constitutes clarity and distinctness, it is this principle, made explicit by Arnauld, which justifies Locke in defining knowledge as the perception of relations of agreement and disagreement of ideas (Locke 1689: IV.1.i) and Hume in treating all mathematics as a matter of the relations of ideas (Hume 1748: section IV). Arnauld's fundamental principle then is:

> All that is contained in the clear and distinct idea of a thing can truly be affirmed of the idea of that thing.
>
> (Arnauld 1964 p. 323)

All such affirmations form starting points (can be taken as axioms) and stand in no need of proof, for nothing could make them more evident or more certain.

Where our ideas are already clear and distinct, in whatever field, then there is no need for proofs. The ideas which are most clearly and distinctly perceived are, for Arnauld, those which are the simplest and most universal, amongst which would be ideas of substance, unity, motion and extension. Arnauld's fundamental principle should not be taken to yield only trivial truths of the 'All bachelors are unmarried' sort (where the definition of 'bachelor' is 'unmarried man'). For example, divisibility may be affirmed of extension and unity may be affirmed of substance even though extension, substance and unity are simple ideas. In other words, what is contained in the clear and distinct perception of an idea is not wholly a result of the complexity of that idea. Descartes argues that an extended substance must be impenetrable, because as an extended substance, one whose extension is essential to its identity, it must occupy a determinate region of space to the exclusion of all other substances. Thus impenetrability is contained in the clear and distinct perception of extended substance. Similarly he argues that the capacity for motion is contained in the idea of extended substance. Impenetrability and capacity for motion in turn contain the idea of being able to be set in motion by impact. Determining what is contained in the clear and distinct perception of an idea is here clearly not a matter of unpacking the components of a definition.

Progress in the acquisition of knowledge is a matter of acquiring clear and distinct ideas of things which are more particular and more complex. In one sense there are no truths which, once known, stand in need of proof. They do not, as regards their content, stand in need of justification. All knowledge and all truths are on the same footing in that, if they are known, they are known intuitively and with immediate (intuitive) certainty. But where the ideas are more complex, clear and distinct perceptions may be lacking, so that we may have to be led, methodically, to an attainment of them. The function of proof, method or reasoning is thus to lead to the formation of clear and distinct ideas and thus to pave the way for knowledge which, once gained as a form of insight, can dispense with the route.

The requirement which Arnauld places on a proof is thus that it proceed in an intuitively intelligible way. Its function is not solely justificatory; rather it is to lead the mind to understanding, to the formation of clear and distinct ideas. The conception underlying the quest for a *method* of discovery is that discoveries attained by following the prescriptions of the method will, for that very reason, come provided with justifications; the *route* to discovery will also provide the justification for any resulting knowledge claims. Each step in a proof is required to be intuitively evident and the steps should form a sequence which is such that it is possible to survey the whole proof to see how and why it leads to its conclusion. The proof as a whole has to be understandable. Mere compulsion of rational assent at each stage is not enough. A proof which produces its conclusion unexpectedly, like a rabbit out of a hat, is not an adequate proof, for it does not yield a deepened understanding of the proposition supposedly proved. This is Arnauld's reason for banning *reductio ad absurdum* proofs; they may convince the mind, he says, but they do not enlighten it, and enlightenment ought to be the principal fruit of knowledge (Arnauld 1964 p. 330). A proof of *not-p* which proceeds by assuming *p* and deriving a contradiction shows us why *p* cannot be true and hence why it would be wrong to assert *p*. But it does not give us grounds for making any assertion in place of *p*.

Suppose $\sqrt{2}$ is a rational number.
Then there are whole numbers p and q such that $\sqrt{2} = p/q$, where p and q have no common factors.
But if $\sqrt{2} = p/q$, $2 = p^2/q^2$ and $2q^2 = p^2$.
Thus p^2 is an even number. But only the square of an even number can be even. So there must be a whole number r such that $p = 2r$.
In which case $2q^2 = 4r^2$ and $q^2 = 2r^2$.
So q^2 must be an even number and so q too must be an even number.
But then both p and q are divisible by 2, contrary to the hypothesis that they have no common factors.
Thus $\sqrt{2}$ cannot be expressed as a fraction and must therefore be an irrational number.

This proof does not shed much light on the nature of $\sqrt{2}$, which would be the reason why someone like Arnauld would not accept it as a proof that $\sqrt{2}$ is an irrational number, for it does not even assure the existence of $\sqrt{2}$. Is $\sqrt{2}$ a number? If so, what sort of number is it? (Compare this with the corresponding question about $\sqrt{-1}$.)

The demand that Arnauld is making on proofs can be traced back to issues which had already been broached by Aristotle in his *Posterior Analytics* (Aristotle 1975), when he noted the difference between deductions which establish facts and those which yield explanations of those facts and hence shed light on the nature of the things involved in them. His example (78a23 ff) involves two valid syllogistic arguments:

(I) The planets do not twinkle.
What does not twinkle is
near.
Therefore, the planets are near.

(II) The planets are near.
What is near does not
twinkle.
Therefore, the planets do not
twinkle.

(I) yields the conclusion *that* the planets are near, whereas (II) demonstrates *why* they do not twinkle. It is not because they do not twinkle that the planets are near, but because they are near that they do not twinkle. Both (I) and (II) are valid deductions and both may have their uses; sometimes we deduce the existence of a cause C from the presence of its effect E. But before being able to do this we have to establish that C is a possible cause of E and that it is the only possible cause given the other circumstances of the occurrence of E. In other words, in the order of understanding, demonstrations which yield explanations have priority. Paying attention only to deductive validity it would be possible, by choosing the wrong starting points, to put things in a deductive order which was quite unexplanatory and hence yielded no under-standing, for those demonstrations which constitute explanations are what yield increased understanding of the natures of the things explained. Again Aristotle gives an example (93b8–15):

> Thunder is noise in the clouds.
> Fire (lightning) is extinguished in the clouds.
> The extinction of fire makes a noise.
> Therefore there is a noise in the clouds (i.e. thunder).

This makes possible an answer to the question 'Why is there thunder?' – 'Because the fire in the clouds (lightning) is being extinguished.' It also makes possible a better account of thunder, one which is not just a verbal definition. 'What is thunder?' – 'The noise of fire being extinguished in the clouds.' The proof does not have as its conclusion 'Thunder is the noise of fire being extin-guished in the clouds'. But acceptance of the proof as giving the cause of thunder also commits one to a revision of the definition of thunder (the formation of a more clear and distinct idea). There is something shown by the explanation which is not deductively proved.

For Aristotle, as for Euclid, explanatory deductions, which are the goal in all sciences since they yield understanding (knowledge of causes), are grounded ultimately in accounts of the natures of the things with which the deduction is concerned, plus some first principles which govern the particular domain of enquiry (Euclid's postulates would be the first principles of geometry) and the order to be deductively mapped is the causal order of this domain, an order determined by the natures of the things in it. Neither the natures of things nor the causal order need be immediately obvious to us. However, the seventeenth century rejected the Aristotelian metaphysics of substances, natural kinds, their essences and natures which underlies this conception, in favour of a view according to which classification is a work of the mind of man – a projection of his ideas onto the world. Ideas thus provide the ground for explanation and understanding. So when Arnauld insists that in geometry the 'natural order' should be followed he is insisting that proofs be explanatory (enlightening) as well as deductively valid (something with which neither Aristotle nor Euclid would disagree) but is also assuming that the 'natural order' here is the order which is natural for the human mind, not the order of independently given natures, or essences.

A prerequisite for following the 'natural order' as Arnauld conceives it is that the starting points for proofs must be things which come first in the order of *human* understanding. It is here that empiricists and rationalists characteristically differ; they disagree about what comes first in the order of human understanding and on whether the order of understanding is or is not distinct from the order of experience. Rationalists drew a distinction between the two orders. The order of understanding starts with what is most simple and universal and is thus reflected in an axiomatized mathematical discipline such as geometry; experience, however, starts with the particular and the complex. Empiricists, on the other hand, claim that all knowledge and all ideas are grounded in the particularity of experience; experience in the guise of sense perception furnishes simple ideas of particular sensed qualities. This means that whilst rationalists and empiricists are agreed that knowledge is a matter of the relation of ideas they do not agree about the role of deduction in the acquisition of knowledge. Descartes quite explicitly sought a method of discovery through reason, starting with the simple and the universal, which would unite the logical with the epistemological foundations of knowledge. It is this which forms the basis of Arnauld's strictures on geometrical proofs – they are to be the vehicle of discovery as well as of justification; axioms and definitions must therefore be epistemological as well as logical starting points. Although the empiricists followed Descartes in his rejection of Aristotelian logic, they clearly could not subscribe to this unification of epistemological with logical foundations. Epistemologically we must start with experience, and as Hume was to spell out most clearly, there is no rationally (deductively) assured route from the particularity of experience to the universality of theoretical knowledge. Thus the impact of the mathematical, intuitive image of reason is very different depending on whether it is set against the background of empiricist or rationalist views. The empiricist is obliged to separate deductive reasoning and justification from the process of discovery and the acquisition of ideas, whereas the rationalist wishes to unite them. The empiricist sees reason and mathematics as tracing connections between ideas which we ourselves have formed in some non-rational process or by explicit definition; it provides a means of systematizing and organizing experience, facilitating prediction, but is not, and cannot be, a source of assured knowledge of the empirical world or of any mind-independent reality. The rationalist, however, sees in mathematics a source of knowledge. Its starting point lies in ideas which are intrinsic to reason, which are neither derived from experience nor arbitrarily constructed by us but which are given along with our rational capacities. Reason is thus a source of enlightenment, a means of transcending the purely experiential, empirical perspective. In neither case was the natural order of understanding presumed to be *merely* the order of the human mind. On the one hand the order inherent in the natural light of reason (the innate intuitive faculty) was assumed to correspond to an objective order. Reason being that of God in every man is guaranteed as a source of divinely objective (transcendent) knowledge. On the other hand, the order of perceptions given in experience, because it is given, not voluntarily imposed, was presumed to reflect, albeit in a manner which is dependent on human sensory capacities, the objective order of the empirical world (which may only be a world of appearances).

The seventeenth century had turned away both from the unaided senses and from distortions imposed by language and tradition to seek a newly objective knowledge in clear, undistorted apprehension of relations between ideas (whether derived from experience or innate) in the mind, a knowledge which is thus grounded in personal, intellectual experience. The problem faced by those taking the way of ideas was how, without divine intervention (without assuming an especially intimate relation between certain ideas in the human mind and ideas in the mind of God), to explain the possibility of objective knowledge of an external world, or even of other minds. Kant's critical philosophy seemed to provide a solution to the first problem. By going between rationalism and empiricism to the position of an empirical realism which was at the same time a transcendental idealism, Kant was able to offer an explanation of how, and a justification for supposing that, mathematics can be a source of objective knowledge about the empirical world. Kant argued that the very conception of a world as empirically real, as organized in space and time, is one which is a necessary condition of the possibility of thought about ourselves as experiencing subjects, but is also one which is supplied by our own innate rational and intuitive capacities. Mathematics is a synthetic *a priori* discipline in which we learn about the structures of space and time, which are the forms of our intuition. All our experience of the empirical world is ordered in space and time. This means that our ideas of space, time and their forms cannot be derived *from* experience but are *imposed on* it as necessary conditions of the possibility of experience as unified by a subject into experience of an empirical world. The world of experience is still a world of appearance but it is the only world within which our conception of reality can have any content. Kant's doctrine of empirical realism but transcendental idealism was designed to bring reconciliation by doing justice to elements of both rationalist and empiricist positions. On the one hand Kant admits that our scientific knowledge is knowledge only of a world of appearances, empirical reality is human, experiential reality, but at the same time he insists that not all ideas are derived from experience; experience is itself a product of the imposition of an order and structure which is inherent in the mind which conceives itself as the subject of experience. On this account mathematical reasoning does give us assured knowledge of the structure of the empirical world because mathematical principles underlie the mental processes by which experience is constituted as experience of an external empirical reality. Mathematical reasoning is not thereby assured as a source of transcendent knowledge, knowledge of a mind-independent reality.

THE RETURN TO EUCLIDEAN STANDARDS

By the late nineteenth century the intellectual climate which produced Darwin and Freud was strongly against the presumption that whatever innate faculties man has could come with any guarantees suiting them to be sources of objective knowledge, even of the empirical world, or of enlightenment. They were more likely to be sources of deception and superstition. With good reason, intuition was being regarded with suspicion in mathematics itself. Nineteenth century developments in mathematics had begun to make it very clear that, whatever intuitions had served earlier mathematicians, they were inadequate as a basis for resolving problems arising out of the newer mathematics. These problems were of two kinds.

(a) There were problems surrounding the infinitesimal calculus and analysis. In particular there were the so-called 'pathological functions', functions which could be algebraically expressed but whose graphs could not be drawn or imagined (for example, functions which are everywhere discontinuous, or functions having infinitely many oscillations between any two points in a given interval). The need here was to develop a secure framework for handling infinite series and functions expressed by use of them. It is all too easy, having once admitted the infinite and the infinitesimal, to produce paradoxes and even apparently to prove absurd results. But calculus, from its first formulation by Newton and Leibniz, was far too useful to discard. Yet without secure foundations, without clear standards of what does and does not constitute a proof of, for example, the existence of a limit of an infinite series, there would remain a question about its reliability. How could one be sure that by using this mathematical style of reasoning in physics one was not liable to draw false conclusions from correct premises. Thus Frege says:

> Later developments, however, have shown more and more clearly that in mathematics a mere moral conviction, supported by a mass of successful applications, is not good enough. Proof is now demanded of many things that formerly passed as self-evident. Again and again the limits of the validity of a proposition have been in this way established for the first time.
>
> (Frege 1950 p. 1e)

(b) There were new symbols being introduced together with calculi employing them, symbols claiming the right to be called numbers – real numbers, imaginary numbers, complex numbers, transfinite ordinal and cardinal numbers. The decision as to whether to recognize these calculi as legitimate new branches of mathematics raised, in an acute form, philosophical questions about the nature of mathematics in general and about the nature of numbers in particular. What is a number? Can there be infinite numbers? What would count as ground for accepting them as possible objects of mathematical investigation? What is required before a set of symbols together with rules for manipulating them becomes a genuine part of mathematics? Acceptance of these new 'numbers' as numbers would certainly require earlier intuitions about numbers to be put aside. Neither complex numbers nor infinite numbers behave in exactly the way that ordinary numbers do – the rules for calculating with them cannot be quite the same and their behaviour is to this extent counter-intuitive. Frege was by no means the only mathematician discussing questions about the nature of numbers. Peano, Dedekind, Cantor and others were also concerned with this problem which was not soluble simply by appeal to intuition or to a 'natural order' of human understanding. Nor could it be straightforwardly resolved by resorting to explicitly conventional definitions, since one could not be sure that these would not yield unwelcome surprises in the form of contradictions or paradoxes. The notion of a function had been defined, but that had not meant that there were no surprises in store or that the definition would never need revision; mathematical reasoning as conducted from the seventeenth through the nineteenth century had certainly not proved to be a trivial matter of unpacking analytic truths from explicit definitions.

Nevertheless, debate of the kind sparked off here was sufficient to expose the inadequacies of grounding claims to objective knowledge in intuition. It is all too easy to claim that something is obviously or self-evidently true, when in fact it is false. There were once plenty of people prepared to claim as self-evident truths that the earth does not move, or that there cannot be a vacuum. What seems obvious to one person from one culture and one historical period may not be at all obvious to a person from another. The problem about a situation where fundamental principles are claimed to be known by intuition is that, being incapable of further proof, it becomes a matter of either you see the truth or you do not; there can be no further relevant rational debate. The doubter is characterized as blind (lacking the relevant intuitive faculty) whereas he sees his opponent as dogmatic, conceited and deluded in thinking that he has a special insight. Disagreements over fundamental truths thought to be known by intuition turn rapidly either into acrimonious and unedifying slanging matches or into polite but interminable debates.

Thus from diverse directions there was a cumulative pressure to rethink and reconceptualize the nature of mathematics and the association between mathematics and reason. If reliance on intuition were to be banished from mathematics there seemed to be only two options open – formalism and logicism. Both of these deny that mathematics starts from a *knowledge* of first principles which have a special mathematical content. Formalism denies that mathematics has the status of a body of knowledge at all; rather, it is just a set of symbols plus rules for manipulating them (a formal calculus) which can be used to facilitate reasoning in other fields. The only requirement on a formal calculus is that it be reliable, that its use not lead to the drawing of false conclusions from true premises and that it not distort the data it is used to record and systematize. Logicism, on the other hand, is a reductive thesis. The claim is that the only fundamental principles to which appeal need be made in mathematics are in fact logical principles – i.e. principles which are not specific to mathematics but which apply within all areas of rational discourse. Thus Frege's claim about arithmetic is that all arithmetic truths can be derived from definitions by appeal only to logical laws. Here we find a return to the Aristotelian/Euclidean standard which required clear demarcations between disciplines; arithmetic has to be founded on the definitions of arithmetical terms and no other notions can be imported for the purposes of developing proofs. Further, there are to be no specifically arithmetic axioms; arithmetic has no first principles to call its own and can thus dispense fully with any appeals to arithmetic intuition. Yet this in itself would not be an advance if logical principles themselves had to be grounded in intuition. Thus the other integral component of the logicist position is an insistence that the laws of logic are laws of truth, not merely of thought. The laws are themselves to be justified by reference to an account of meaning, of the way in which language functions as the vehicle for objective knowledge, not by reference either to an account of the way the human mind works or by appeal to rational faculties of any kind. Although there is no move back to Aristotelian metaphysics, there is here a move back to thinking of proofs as required to reflect an order which is independent of and external to individual human minds.

For Arnauld, as for Descartes, Locke and Hume, the meaning of a word is given by the idea for which it stands. The association between word and idea is arbitrary. Relations between ideas are non-arbitrary, being grounded in the nature of the ideas related, and in this sense they are objective. Knowledge thus becomes a matter of correctly judging these relations. However, as Frege complained, this makes knowledge incommunicable; it becomes a strictly individual and private affair, for a person can only hear or read the *words* of another; he cannot observe the ideas for which they purportedly stand. He has therefore no assurance that what he understands by a word is what his interlocutor meant by it. Yet the whole point about objective knowledge is that it is public knowledge, in principle accessible to all.

> If the content of the sentence '2 + 3 = 5' is exactly the same, in the strictest sense, for all those who recognise it to be true, this means that it is not a product of the mind of this person and a product of the mind of that person, but that it is grasped and recognised as true by both equally. Even if subjective elements are a necessary part and parcel of this grasping of a concept, we shall not include them in what we call 'true'.
>
> (Frege 1950 p. 4)

In trying to secure the individual's right to claim knowledge on his own account and so free him from subservience to an externally imposed, institutional authority, the seventeenth-century movement left the nineteenth century with the opposite predicament in which knowledge seemed to have no life external to the individual.

The depth of Frege's opposition to what has come to be called 'psychologism', the approach to logic and knowledge which treats logic as the art of thinking and knowledge as concerned with relations between ideas, cannot be over-emphasized. It is the opposition on which Frege's own position is founded. For example he says:

28

We suppose, it would seem, that concepts sprout in the individual mind like leaves on a tree, and we think to discover their nature by studying their birth; we seek to define them psychologically, in terms of the nature of the human mind. But this account makes everything subjective and if we follow it through to the end we do away with truth.

(Frege 1950 p. viie)

Frege will then turn the tables not merely on Arnauld, but on all the various inheritors of the way of ideas.

To insist on this point Frege lays down three fundamental principles which, in his view, should govern any philosophical enquiry into the nature of arithmetic. The first of these is:

Always to separate sharply the psychological from the logical, the subjective from the objective.

(Frege 1950 p. xe)

The starting points for a proof of a theorem should not be confused with the mental or psychological conditions which have to be satisfied before a person can construct or understand the proof. So, unlike Arnauld, Frege cites with approval Euclid's tendency to give proofs where anyone would agree to the proposition without proof.

The aim of proof is, in fact, not merely to place the truth of a proposition beyond all doubt, but also to afford us insight into the dependence of one truth upon another. After we have convinced ourselves that a boulder is immovable, by trying unsuccessfully to move it, there remains the further question, what is it that supports it so securely?

(Frege 1950 p. 2e)

In other words, indubitability, Cartesian clear and distinct perception which has resisted methodical doubt, is not enough. We must ask for an explanation, which is not a psychological but a logical explanation of why this is a truth (if indeed it is). Proof is demanded even of those things which seem self-evident. The starting points, arithmetical and geometrical first principles (axioms), will not be the starting points for knowledge (epistemological foundations) but must be the ultimate grounds of truth/proof (logical foundations). In the absence of divine guarantees for our innate rational faculties, it cannot be presumed that these two kinds of foundation will coincide. We should note that what Frege and Arnauld disagree about is not that proofs should do more than put propositions beyond doubt; they disagree over what more is required of a proof, over the nature of knowledge, and hence over what will constitute well-founded knowledge.

Logic, as dealing with the principles of the dependence of truths upon one another, cannot now be seen as an *art*, a technique for employing a human intuitive faculty. It must now be a *science* concerned with objective relations between the contents of statements. Logical principles are laws of truth, not laws of thought. Logic and reason must be externalized if they are to play a role in the acquisition and justification of objective knowledge – knowledge of something which exists independently of individual human minds and which cannot thus itself be the private property of an individual mind. Objective knowledge is public knowledge and exactly how to account for the possibility of public knowledge, in particular in the case of mathematics, which is not dealing directly with concrete physical objects, remains one of the central concerns of philosophers of mathematics, a problem to which Frege and Russell both attempted solutions. Both attack the problem by putting language in the foreground, for it is in language that knowledge finds public expression and it is via language that knowledge is communicated from one person to another. Language thus serves to mediate between the individual knower and the independent thing known (the object of knowledge). But this can be the case only if the suggestion that words acquire meaning by being made to stand for ideas in the mind of each individual language user is wrong. Frege's search for the logical foundations of arithmetic thus also had to be a quest for an account of the meanings of the sentences in which arithmetical statements are made. Frege's second fundamental principle thus concerns meaning:

> Never to ask for the meaning of a word in isolation, but only in the context of a proposition.
>
> (Frege 1950 p. xe)

Here Frege comments that if this principle is not observed

> one is almost forced to take as the meanings of words, mental pictures or acts of the individual mind, and so to offend against the first principle as well.
>
> (Frege 1950 p. xe)

This principle has very far-reaching consequences for the whole conception of knowledge and reason employed not just by Frege but by all those working within the framework supplied by his logic. Closely associated with this principle, but in a way which will become clear only in the more detailed discussion of chapter 2, is Frege's third fundamental principle:

Never to lose sight of the distinction between concept and object.

(Frege 1950 p. xe)

Thus, whilst deductive organization leading to axiomatization represents an ideal of rigour which must be endorsed in principle by anyone recognizing mathematics as a discipline in which claims must be backed by proofs, it is clear that there is room for philosophical dispute about the standards of rigour to be incorporated into this ideal. Views on standards of rigour relate closely to views on the aims of proof, and on the nature of knowledge and hence on the order to be reflected in an axiomatization. As we have seen, Frege and Arnauld hold different views. For Arnauld the aim is *enlightenment*, or understanding; for Frege it is justified knowledge of *truth*. For Arnauld the order sought is the order of learning or understanding in which the first principles are those which are epistemologically fundamental. For Frege the order sought is an objective, logical order in which the first principles are those which are logically fundamental – those from which all further truths of the discipline can be deduced and which cannot themselves be deduced from anything more fundamental. The order here is that of formal deductive justification from which appeals to intuition have been removed and is opposed to what Frege sees as the subjective order of discovery, the order in which things become intelligible to us. His three fundamental principles are designed continually to put one on one's guard against the intrusion of subjective, psychological considerations.

However, it may turn out that the contrast is not as clear cut as it might seem: that this dispute here is more rhetorical than real, that it is a dispute as much about an image of reason as about the realities of good mathematical practice. For the time being we may simply note that Arnauld presumes that the order he *imposes* on his ideas on the basis of essentially subjective criteria reflects an objective order amongst those things represented by his ideas, for only on this assumption can he claim this order to be the order of understanding, of enlightenment concerning what is represented in his ideas. Frege, on the other hand, presumes that the logical ordering of truths is *discoverable* and will lead to a deeper understanding of the truths ordered. Only on this assumption does his project have a point. But in Frege's view the route to a fuller understanding of the nature of any class of statements can only go via a deliberate putting aside of all subjective, psychological considerations. This is in itself a thesis about the correct route to the acquisition of a certain kind of knowledge.

2

FREGE: ARITHMETIC
AS LOGIC

No sharp boundary can be drawn between logic and arithmetic. ... If this formal theory is correct, then logic cannot
be as barren as it may appear upon superficial examination
– an appearance for which logicians themselves must be
assigned part of the blame.

(Frege 1971 p. 142)

In his work on logic and arithmetic Frege had two inter-related
aims: (i) to characterize the reasoning procedures used in the
numerical branches of mathematics, and (ii) to give an account of
the nature of mathematical knowledge concerning numbers and
numerical functions. The first project led to his *Begriffsschrift*
(Frege 1879, 1972), a system of formal logical notation and rules of
inference. Although Frege's actual notation was never adopted
(the symbolism now in use owes more to the notation used by
Peano and Russell) the crucial revisions in logic which it embodied
form the basis of most of the systems currently in use and it
would be difficult to over-emphasize their importance. The second
project was presented in a non-formal manner in *Die Grundlagen
der Arithmetik* (Frege 1884, 1950). The two are brought together
in his *Grundgesetze der Arithmetik* (Frege 1893, 1964).

CALCULATION AND REASONING

It had long been recognized that mathematical reasoning, especially the increasingly complex numerical reasoning involved in
analysis, could not be represented adequately by syllogistic logic.
It was the development of analytic geometry which gave added
force to Descartes' rejection of (Aristotelian) logic. Algebraic

reasoning involves the manipulation of equations and inequalities and the expression and manipulation of functions. Its validity often rests on the correct application of procedures for transforming expressions. For example

> Consider the function $f(x) = 4x - 4x^2$.
> Since $4x - 4x^2 = 4x(1 - x)$, we can easily see that $f(x)$ will take the value 0 when $x = 0$ and when $x = 1$.

Here it is not a matter of dealing with relations between general terms (which can be handled using syllogisms) but of applying functions or operations to individual arguments and of establishing relationships between functions by establishing general relations between their values over a given range of arguments. It seems that the reasoning concerns particulars and yet it is used to obtain generally applicable results. This had led Kant, amongst others, to characterize mathematical reasoning by saying that it sees the universal in the particular, rather than deriving the particular from the universal as is the case in logically deductive reasoning. Since particulars are presented to intuition, this forms part of his justification for claiming that mathematical reasoning, by using a special form of intuition, goes beyond any formal logical reasoning and for endorsing that part of the Cartesian position which recognizes and emphasizes an intuitive component in our deductive, rational faculties. Frege's elimination of reliance on intuition thus requires him to show that formal logic can be extended so as to embrace reasoning about particulars and the transition between this and universal claims.

To accomplish this Frege drew heavily on the mathematical notion of a function, extending it into the realm of logic. The power of the mathematical notion and its notation lies precisely in its ability to mediate the transition from individual arguments and values to the function conceived as establishing a relation between the totality of arguments in its domain and the set of values which constitute its range. So, for example, we could for any real number compute the value of the simple function, $f(x) = 4x - 4x^2$, introduced above: $f(0.5) = 1$ and $f(1) = 0$. But we can also argue that for any value of x such that $1 \geqslant x \geqslant 0$, $f(x)$ always takes a value between 0 and 1, i.e. $1 \geqslant f(x) \geqslant 0$, and we can recognize this function to be one whose graph is a parabola.

We can prove things about the parabola (the totality of related arguments and values of the function) by studying the individual

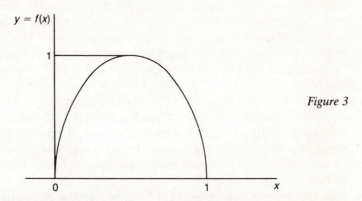

Figure 3

values taken by $f(x)$ together with the general constraints placed on these by its definition. A function is applied to individual numbers as arguments and produces a constant, algebraically characterized, relation between arguments and values which is determined by the definition of the function. This makes it possible to make general assertions about the values of the function or about the characteristics of its graph.

Frege extends this notation of function and argument, together with its accompanying patterns of inference, to concepts (Kant (1929: A106) had already insisted that the application of a concept to an object is a matter of the application of a rule). Here it is important to stress the difference between a function and a number, a difference which is to be transferred to illuminate the distinction between a concept and an object. A function is the expression of a rule determining the value of the function for a given argument. It is something incomplete in that we understand it only in relation to its application to numbers to yield values and the expression for a function reflects this by using the variable 'x' as a place holder for the name of a number. Similarly a concept is said to be incomplete; a concept is something which is to be applied to an object to yield a truth value. Numbers, and objects in general, are, on the other hand, said to be complete and self-subsistent. The judgement that the object by my right hand is a mug of coffee now becomes an assertion of the form 'mug of coffee (a) = True' , where 'a' stands for the object by my right hand and 'True' stands for one of the two possible 'truth values'. So the judgement is that it is correct to apply the concept '... is a mug of coffee' to a, i.e. the rules for applying the concept (smell, taste, appearance . . .) yield the value True. To apply that same concept to the object in my left hand (which happens to be a pen) would yield the value False. In other words, concepts become functions which take individual objects as arguments and always have as values one of the two truth values, True or False. The general notation for a concept $(F(x), G(y))$, like that for any function, will employ a variable, 'x' or 'y'. This marks a departure from the traditional Aristotelian way of reading singular statements as assertions to the effect that a particular kind of relation holds between a subject term and a predicate term, a relation expressed by the copula 'is', giving, for example, the structure '(a) is (mug of coffee)'.

In addition it is now possible for Frege to view the propositional connectives 'and' , 'or', 'not', 'if . . . then', whose behaviour was familiar as a result of Boole's algebraic approach to propositional logic, as truth functions, i.e. as functions which for truth values as arguments give truth values as values. Thus p & q = True if, and only if, p = True and q = True and is False otherwise. 'If p then q' (or p $\rightarrow$ q) = False if, and only if, p = True and q = False and is True otherwise.

The power of the functional notation lies in its ability to yield a representation of the relation between singular and general statements. Mathematics provided Frege with examples of operators which take functions as arguments and yield numbers as values. One such operator would be that of taking the definite integral from 0 to 1. Applying this to our previously introduced function we would have the following.

$$\int_0^1 f(x) \ dx = \int_0^1 4x - 4x^2 \ dx = \tfrac{2}{3}$$

Here the value $\tfrac{2}{3}$ depends on no single value of $4x - 4x^2$, but on all the infinitely many values it takes for arguments between 0 and 1. Since, for any given object as argument, a concept can only take one or other of the two truth values, the only sort of statement which could be made about its values over a given domain of arguments would have to be concerned with the distribution of Trues and Falses over this domain. This forms the basis for the introduction of the universal and existential quantifiers, '$\forall x$' and '$\exists x$'. Frege introduces these as second level concepts, i.e. concepts which take a concept as argument and yield a truth value. Thus

$\forall x\ F(x)$ = True   if and only if $F(a)$ = True for every object a.
$\exists x\ F(x)$ = True   if and only if   there is an object a for which
$$F(a) = \text{True}.$$

It is also possible to introduce other, numerically definite quantifiers, but they can be defined in terms of the two quantifiers already given. Thus, for example.

$$\exists x_1\ F(x) \equiv_{df} \exists x\ (F(x)\ \&\ \forall y\ (F(y) \rightarrow x = y)).$$

Statements of the form 'All Fs are G', which figured so prominently in syllogistic logic, now receive a new representation. They are no longer seen as expressing a relation between terms, or a relation between the extensions of terms, but as saying that the complex concept 'If x is F, then x is G' (or $Fx \rightarrow Gx$) takes the value True for every object, i.e. $\forall x\ (Fx \rightarrow Gx)$.

The effect of this analogical extension of mathematical notation and its associated procedures for reasoning with and about functions carries with it the strong impression that reasoning in general is being reduced to calculation – calculation with truth values instead of numbers – and thus that effectively we have a reduction of logic to mathematics, of all reasoning to 'numerical' calculatory reasoning. However, at this point Frege turns around to effect a reduction in the reverse direction. Having extended the expressive power and flexibility of formal logic by drawing heavily on the mathematical notion of a function and the reasoning procedures associated with it, he then proceeds to reduce all functions to truth functions, and hence to reduce all distinctively numerical reasoning to reasoning which could be handled by the laws for 'calculating' with truth values. The key here is that having once accepted the underlying function–concept analogy there is no reason to resist the further analogy between functions of several arguments and relations, between for example $f(x,y) = x + y$ and $R(x,y) \equiv$ 'x is the father of y'. Relations will be functions of two (or more) arguments whose values are always truth values. But then, for any numerical function $f(x)$, of a single argument, there will be a corresponding relation, $R_f(x,y) \equiv_{df} y = f(x)$. It thus seems possible that all reasoning involving and concerning numerical functions might be reducible to reasoning involving only these corresponding relations, and hence that numerical reasoning could be subsumed under the more general framework of relational reasoning, for which Aristotelian logic provided no framework but which can be accommodated in Frege's extended formal framework. From this standpoint the claim that arithmetic does not require distinctive arithmetical reasoning procedures at least looks plausible. Numerical calculation may be reducible to a generic 'calculation' with truth values (a species of binary computation). In which case, if logical laws are regarded as laws of truth rather than laws of human thought procedures, they should be expressible as rules governing this kind of 'truth–value calculation'.

NUMBERS AND THE NATURE OF ARITHMETICAL TRUTHS

Frege claimed that all true arithmetic statements, i.e. all true statements about the positive whole numbers 0, 1, 2, 3, ..., are analytic truths. That is, not only can they be proved using formal, logical methods by appeal only to strictly arithmetical principles and concepts (the Euclidean standard of rigour), but also there is in fact no need to appeal to any distinctively arithmetic first principles; the only principles required are those of logic. It is here that Frege goes beyond Euclidean standards of rigour, aiming to eliminate entirely the need to appeal to intuition. If there are no distinctively arithmetic first principles, then there is no need to appeal to an intuitive rational faculty ('numerical intuition') as that which assures us of their truth. Frege did not claim that the whole of mathematics can dispense with intuition, for he allowed that geometry, concerned as it was with the structure of space and time, had to rest on specifically geometrical principles whose truth could only be recognized by appeal to intuitions of space and time.

In stating his position Frege uses terminology introduced by Kant, but interpreted in his own way. Kant had claimed that all mathematical truths (by which he understood those of geometry and arithmetic) are synthetic *a priori* truths. This classifies mathematical truth on the basis of two distinctions which Kant introduced, that between analytic and synthetic judgements, and that between *a priori* and *a posteriori* truths. Kant defined these as follows:

> *An analytic judgement* is one in which the predicate B belongs to the subject A, as something which is (covertly) contained in the concept A. ... adds nothing through the

predicate to the concept of the subject, but merely breaks it up into those constituent concepts that have all along been thought in it, although confusedly. A *synthetic judgement* is one which adds to the concept of the subject a predicate which has not been in any wise thought in it, and which no analysis could possibly extract from it.

(A7 B11)

Thus it is evident: 1. that through analytic judgements our knowledge is not in any way extended, and that the concept which I have is merely set forth and made intelligible to me; 2. that in synthetic judgements I must have besides the concept of the subject, something else (X), upon which the understanding may rely, if it is to know that a predicate, not contained in this concept nevertheless belongs to it.

(Kant 1929 A8)

Kant classified the judgement that all bodies are extended as analytic, and the judgement that all bodies are heavy as synthetic.

A posteriori knowledge is knowledge which can only be derived from experience, whereas *a priori* knowledge is knowledge which can be acquired without being derived from experience. Correct analytic judgements will clearly yield *a priori* knowledge, since analytic judgements are grounded in the concepts involved rather than in experience of things falling under those concepts. In the case of a synthetic judgement, everything depends on the nature of the X which grounds it. Where X is experience, the knowledge will be *a posteriori* and will be synthetic *a posteriori*, or empirical, knowledge. But Kant also insisted that X may be something which is not derived *from* experience but is, on the contrary, a *necessary condition of* experience. For example, all experience is assumed to take place in time, to occupy time, and to be ordered in a single, linear time sequence. The notion of time itself cannot therefore be derived from experience, but is a condition of there being any experience which is thought of as lasting a certain amount of time and as forming part of a temporal sequence. This sort of knowledge of time is therefore synthetic *a priori* knowledge, grounded in a pure *a priori* intuition of time – a sense of time which must precede any experience (where experience is being taken as empirical knowledge, i.e. conceptualized experience about which judgements are made, as distinct from the experience as the sort of sensory awareness of young babies and animals). Kant claimed that all mathematical knowledge is ultimately grounded in *a priori* intuitions of space and time and that it is thus synthetic *a priori* knowledge. He also admitted the possibility of synthetic *a priori* philosophical knowledge derived from concepts such as substance, cause, unity, which, he argued, must be given *a priori*; they too cannot be derived from experience because they are presupposed by it and are necessary conditions of its possibility.

This Kantian view of mathematics, which provides for grounding in intuition, is the target of attack for all those mathematicians urging the elimination of appeals to intuition in mathematics. However, whereas there were those who, like Russell, attacked the whole conception of synthetic *a priori* knowledge, Frege did not do this. He was concerned only to dispute Kant's view of arithmetic. In setting out his position, Frege took over Kant's terminology with apparently only minor variations. The question of deciding the status of a mathematical proposition

> ... becomes, in fact, that of finding the proof of the proposition, and of following it up right back to the primitive truths. If in carrying out this process, we come only on general logical laws and on definitions, then the truth is an analytic one, bearing in mind that we must also take account of all propositions upon which the admissibility of any of the definitions depends. If, however, it is impossible to give the proof without making use of truths which are not of a general logical nature, but belong to the sphere of some special science, then the proposition is a synthetic one. For a truth to be *a posteriori*, it must be impossible to construct a proof of it without including an appeal to facts, i.e. to truths which cannot be proved and are not general, since they contain assertions about particular objects. But if, on the contrary, its proof can be derived exclusively from general laws, which themselves neither need nor admit of proof, then the truth is *a priori*.

> (Frege 1950 4e)

In other words we have:

Analytic truth   can be proved from general logical laws and definitions alone.

Synthetic truth   cannot be proved without making use of truths which are not of a general logical nature, but belong to the sphere of some special science.

A posteriori truth   cannot be proved without including an appeal to facts, assertions about particular objects.

A priori truth   can be proved from exclusively general laws, which themselves neither need nor admit of proof.

These definitions still allow for the possibility of synthetic *a priori* knowledge. It would be knowledge grounded in the general laws of some specific science, such as the axioms for Euclidean geometry, where these are known to be true and it is clear that the demand for further proof would be inappropriate. Frege then argued, quite plausibly, that arithmetic cannot be a special science with its own first principles because it, like logic, has unlimited applicability; wherever we can distinguish objects, or units, of any kind we can start counting, adding, subtracting etc. We can even count numbers themselves as when we say that there are two prime numbers between three and ten. The domain of arithmetic is nothing less than everything thinkable (Frege 1950 p. 14). Thus its principles cover the same domain as those of logic and seemed, to Frege, to be intimately connected with them. Here again Frege is not departing radically from Kant's position. Kant by no means denied the applicability of arithmetic to all that is thinkable. His claim about the character of mathematics in general was that it deals with quantities (arithmetic is the science of discrete quantity and geometry the science of continuous quantities) and that the only way in which we can arrive at a knowledge of general principles for quantitative (as opposed to qualitative) reasoning is via a construction of exemplars in *a priori* intuition using the creative powers of the productive imagination. Thus, for example, to appreciate the universal truth of $7 + 5 = 12$ we cannot use logic.

> The concept of 12 is by no means already thought in merely thinking this union of 7 and 5; and I may analyze my concept of such a possible sum as long as I please, still I shall never find the 12 in it.
>
> (Kant 1929 B15)

Instead in imagination we might construct a sequence of seven identical units and proceed to add one unit to this five times over, counting the running total as we go. This could be done on paper too, but only on the understanding that the process is symbolic of an abstract, non-empirical process. Our concern is not with the particular marks but with the units they symbolize. Kant's claim was that in the case of quantitative reasoning we have to derive general principles from reasoning about abstract particulars (presented in pure intuition), whereas logic only allows for deduction from general principles to particular instances.

NUMBERS AS OBJECTS

The core of Frege's rejection of the Kantian position and its appeal to intuition has therefore nothing to do with the scope of the application of arithmetic but has to do with the character of arithmetical reasoning on the one hand and with the nature of numbers on the other. Frege wished to deny any distinction in kind between qualitative and quantitative reasoning, between reasoning in accordance with formal logical principles and quantitative arithmetical reasoning (calculating). His strategy for achieving this aim was outlined in the previous section. The simplest strategy that the logicist might adopt would be to argue that twoness is like redness – a characteristic shared by all pairs of objects and thus something which can be assimilated to a quality. Indeed we have already seen that numerical predicates can be given purely logical definitions. We have:

There are no Fs $\quad \equiv_{df} \exists_0 x\, F(x)$
$\quad\quad\quad\quad\quad \equiv_{df} \forall x\, \neg F(x)$

There is exactly one F $\quad \equiv_{df} \exists_1 x\, F(x)$
$\quad\quad\quad\quad\quad \equiv_{df} \exists x\, (F(x)\ \&\ \forall y\, (F(y) \to y = x))$

There are exactly two Fs $\quad \equiv_{df} \exists_2 x\, F(x)$
$\quad\quad\quad\quad\quad \equiv_{df} \exists_1 x\, (F(x)\ \&\ \exists_1 y\, (F(y)\ \&\ y \neq x))$

There are exactly three Fs $\quad \equiv_{df} \exists_3 x\, F(x)$
$\quad\quad\quad\quad\quad \equiv_{df} \exists_1 x\, (F(x)\ \&\ \exists_2 y\, (F(y)\ \&\ y \neq x))$

and so on.

However, knowing in what circumstances it is correct to say that there are three goats in the field does not give a basis for being able to say that $3 = 2 + 1$ (no more than knowing that these tulips are red gives a basis for knowing that red and blue make purple). In other words, the use of numbers in concrete, counting situations, or in application to any given domain of objects, is not yet arithmetic. There is an abstractive step which has yet to be made to go from counting particular collections to performing calculations which establish relations between numbers, calculations whose results can be used and relied upon in any application. This is analogous to the step which has to be made when shifting from describing things using colour words to talking about colours, their interrelationships and properties. If we are going to abide by the distinction between concept and object, then having defined number concepts does not yet give us numbers. In syllogistic logic this problem does not arise in the same form because there it is allowed that a term may occupy either subject or predicate position. From Plato to Kant and Cantor the abstractive step which takes us to numbers had been conceived as made possible by a transition from collections of concrete individuals to collections of abstract units, units having no qualities beyond their discreteness and distinctness from one another and which are hence all alike. Collections of such units then provide standard, abstract examples (paradigms or forms) denoted by numerical symbols and against which rules for calculation can be checked by thinking in terms of manipulations of collections of abstract units. Appeal to intuition is required precisely for the apprehension of these schematic entities, whether they are thought to be eternal forms (Plato), constructions in pure intuition (Kant) or products of a double abstraction from experience (Cantor).

Frege neither denied that arithmetic is concerned with numbers nor denied that numbers are abstract objects. In fact he insisted that numbers must be regarded as objects; the number 2 is distinct from any pair of empirically given objects. But equally numbers could not, as far as Frege was concerned, be mental constructs, ideas in the mind of any individual human being. What he had to argue was that reasoning about numbers does not need to be grounded in their construction in pure intuition; it can be grounded in definitions. It is here, then, with the notion of an object, what it takes to define an object, and the relation between concept and object that we seem to get to the heart of the matter, and incidentally to understand why Frege included his third injunction (see p. 31) – never to lose sight of the distinction between concept and object. It is this distinction which is crucial to Frege's claims about the nature of numbers and to the logical framework which he developed in order to substantiate his claim concerning the character of arithmetical reasoning. Frege had to show that it is possible to define an *object*. Kant implicitly assumed that it is only possible to define a *concept* of an object – to give a descriptive identification of it, a rule by which we would recognize the object. An object as such has to be presented in intuition, either empirically when we experience it, or when we construct it in imagination either reproductively as in memory or productively when we imagine things of which we have had no experience. To this Frege retorts

§104 ... Have we really no right to speak of $1000^{1000^{1000}}$ until such time as that many objects have been given to us in intuition? Is it, till then, an empty symbol? Not at all. It has a perfectly definite sense, even though, psychologically speaking and having regard to the shortness of human life, it is impossible for us ever to become conscious of that many objects (a simple calculation shows that millions of years would not be time enough for that); in spite of that $1000^{1000^{1000}}$ is still an object, whose properties we can come to know, even though it is not intuitable. To convince ourselves of this, we only have to show, introducing the symbol a^n for the nth power of a, that for positive integral a and n this expression always refers to one and only one positive whole number.

(Frege 1950 p. 114)

What is impressive about the power that arithmetic gives us is precisely that it enables us to reason and calculate with confidence beyond our powers of imagining. Even if presented with a million $1 bills we would not, with any confidence, be sure even by counting that there were exactly a million, rather than 1,000,005 or 999,997, and we certainly couldn't tell just by looking. Yet we could be quite sure that there were either a million there or not and that we know what it would mean to say that. Bankers are quite happy to calculate with millions, basing business transactions on their calculations. Frege is insisting that, if such confidence is justified, intuition alone cannot provide the justification. Rather we need to trust our computational operations, being sure first that they have been well defined and then that they have been correctly carried out. The first condition for being well defined is, as Frege pointed out, that we should be sure, before talking even of 1000^{1000} that exponentiation has been defined and that its definition ensures that, for all positive whole numbers a and n, there is a positive whole number satisfying the condition for being a^n and that there cannot be more than one number which does so.

How can this be done? If we think purely in terms of trying to pin down an individual object by giving a very detailed qualitative description of it, we are bound to fail. It always remains (logically) possible that there should be an 'identical twin', an exactly similar but numerically distinct object. So if definitions were restricted to being listings of qualities, it would be impossible to meet Frege's demand. As Frege himself pointed out (Frege 1950 p. 100), this is effectively what traditional Aristotelian logic did restrict one to and hence Kant seemed to think of concepts as being defined only by giving a simple list of characteristics. If we represent concepts, or rather the classes of things falling under them, by the areas inside circles (see figure 4), then all we get by combining the concepts A, B and C is a concept ABC which has as its extension the (shaded) region which is common to all three circles, a region whose boundaries are already given by the three concepts.

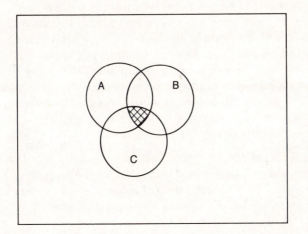

Figure 4

But by extending his logic Frege has greatly extended his powers of definition. For example there are a number of ways in which it is possible to define concepts from a relation $R(x,y)$ by using quantifiers, giving the four distinct concepts $\exists x\ R(x,y)$, $\exists y\ R(x,y)$, $\forall x\ R(x,y)$ and $\forall y\ R(x,y)$. Frege exploits this in giving his definition of the concept of number, which starts with an existential quantifier. Another way of obtaining a concept from a relation is by 'diagonalizing' to give $R(x,x)$ (so called because, if we were thinking of x,y as the co-ordinates of points on the plane, then points with indices x,x would be those on the diagonal line through the origin). It is by doing this to the identity relation that Frege arrived at the concept '$x = x$', and hence also the concept '$x \neq x$' in terms of which he defined 0. Furthermore, once one is thinking in terms of relations it becomes possible to define an expression intended to refer to a unique object which we have never encountered, and may never actually be able to encounter. This can be done if $R(x,y)$ is a relation such that for each x there can only be one y such that $R(x,y)$; then for any object a, 'b = the y such that $R(a,y)$' will be a legitimate way of defining a name for an object. For example let $R(x,y)$ be 'x is the (biological) father of y'. Then, given what we know about the biology of human reproduction, every human being has to have had a father and they can only have had one biological father (precluding here future genetic engineering possibilities). So, provided we are confident of the reference of 'Adolf Hitler', we can be sure that 'the father of Adolf Hitler' also refers to exactly one human being who lived in the past.

This suggests that once it has been proved that there are some numbers, it will be possible to define expressions referring to further numbers via their relations to those already given. The problem for Frege thus reduced to that of how to get going. How could the existence of any numbers be established by logical means alone? Central to his strategy was his insistence that it is only in the context of a sentence that a word has a meaning. Thus, when summarizing his strategy Frege says:

> we must never try to define the meaning of a word in isolation, but only as it is used in the context of a proposition: only by adhering to this can we, as I believe, avoid a physical view of number without slipping into a psychological view of it.

and he continues:

> Now for every object there is one type of proposition which must have a sense, namely the recognition statement, which in the case of numbers is called an identity. ... The problem, therefore, was now this: to fix the sense of a numerical identity, that is, to express that sense without making use of number words or the word 'number'.

> (Frege 1950 §106)

If a name standing on its own could be defined then it would be natural to think that one should be able to point to or otherwise identify an object of which it is the name. But whereas one can point to a person and say, 'That's Abraham Blunt', one cannot point to anything and say 'That's 5'. On the other hand, if we think of the function of a name in a sentence, such as 'Abraham Blunt is a farmer', we recognize that we need to know who or what the name refers to in order to determine whether the sentence is true or false. Frege's proposal was that a name has been defined if one has ensured that every proposition in which it occurs has a determinate truth value, for the defined expression will then be functioning as a name, referring to an object, even if it is not possible to point to that object. In particular, criteria must have been given for determining whether two names are names for the same object. Since natural numbers are the objects about which statements are made in arithmetic, the truth or falsity of arithmetic statements is to be determined by reference to them. So if '$m = n$' is a true numerical identity, an arithmetic sentence containing 'm' should not change its truth value when 'n' is substituted for 'm'. For example, '7 is a prime number' should have the same truth value as '$3 + 4$ is a prime number'. If definitions are given which determine the truth value of every statement about numbers in such a way that this substitution requirement is satisfied, then, Frege argued, this is all that can be required by way of introducing numbers as objects.

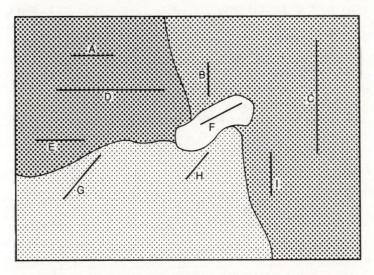

Figure 5 Partition induced by the relation 'is parallel to'

Frege's strategy for providing such definitions rests on the insight that there are relations, such as 'has the same length as' and 'is parallel to', which when applied over a given domain of objects cut it up into classes in such a way that every object in the domain belongs to at least one class and to no more than one class. Such relations induce partitions of the domain.

Such relations are equivalence relations, i.e. they satisfy the following definition.

$R(x,y)$ is an equivalence relation iff

$\forall x\ R(x,x)$	(reflexive)
$\forall x\ \forall y\ (R(x,y) \rightarrow R(y,x))$	(symmetric)
$\forall x\ \forall y\ \forall z\ (R(x,y)\ \&\ R(y,z) \rightarrow R(x,z))$	(transitive).

The classes into which an equivalence relation partitions a domain are then called equivalence classes.

Given the definition:

the direction of A $=_{df}$ the class of lines parallel to A

it can be proved that

the direction of A = the direction of B iff A is parallel to B.

To follow a similar procedure in the case of numbers requires that one find an equivalence relation which can be defined without making reference to numbers and which can be regarded as an explication of what it means to say that the number of Fs is the same as the number of Gs. A way of checking that there are the same number of objects in each of two collections without actually counting (and hence using numbers) is to check that each object from one collection can be paired with exactly one object from the other collection without there being any of the second collection left over (for example, checking that there are the same number of cups as saucers by setting each cup on a saucer and checking that each saucer has a cup on it). When this is possible there is said to be a one–one correspondence between the two collections. This suggests that we should define 'the number of Fs' in such a way that (1) can be proved.

(1)   the number of Fs = the number of Gs iff
      there is a one–one correspondence between the Fs and the Gs.

The requirement on a relation that it be a one–one correspondence can be expressed as a formal, logical requirement, namely:

(2) $R(x,y)$ is a one–one correspondence between the Fs and the Gs $\equiv_{df}$

$$\forall x \ (F(x) \rightarrow \exists_1 y \ (G(y) \ \& \ R(x,y))) \ \&$$
$$\forall y \ (G(y) \rightarrow \exists_1 x \ (F(x) \ \& \ R(x,y))).$$

If two collections are said to be equinumerous whenever there is a one–one correspondence between them, then equinumerosity will be a relation between collections which can be shown to be an equivalence relation and which can be defined using only formal, logical notions. Thus numbers can be defined as equivalence classes under this equivalence relation, i.e.

(3) the number of Fs $=_{df}$ the class of classes X which are equinumerous with the class of Fs.

From this it is then easy to prove (1).

THE NATURAL NUMBERS

But although this in a sense gives numbers and a definition of the concept 'is a number'

(4) x is a number $\equiv_{df}$ there is a concept F such that x is the number of Fs.

it does not give any objects which are plausible candidates for the natural numbers. The task of locating these, however, has been reduced to that of discovering which of the numbers just defined should get the names $0, 1, 2, \ldots$ Clearly we would want it to be the case that

0 = the number of Fs iff there are no Fs

1 = the number of Fs iff there is exactly one thing which is F

and so on.

Since the number of Fs is the class of all classes containing the same number of elements as the class of Fs, all that is required is to be able, for each number, to pick out a class which has just that number of elements. This must be done in such a way that the membership of the selected class is logically determined. Here again Frege showed great ingenuity.

(5) $0 =_{df}$ the number of objects x, such that $x \neq x$.

For any object a, to say that it is not identical to itself is a contradiction. Thus $\neg \exists x \ (x \neq x)$ is a logical truth and it is possible to prove that if a concept $F(x)$ is such that there is a one–one correspondence between the Fs and the things which are not identical with themselves then $\neg\exists x\, F(x)$ must also be true, i.e. the number of Fs will also be 0.

The further definitions required are as follows.

(6) $1 =_{df}$ the number of objects x such that $0 = x$.

(7) $m = n + 1$ (m immediately follows n in the number series) $\equiv_{df}$ there is a concept $F(x)$ such that $m =$ the number of Fs & there is an object c such that $F(c)$ & $n =$ the number of objects y such that $F(y)$ & $y \neq c$.

Definition (7) is only legitimate if it can be proved that there can be at most one number which immediately follows any given number. So it has to be proved that if m and k both come immediately after n in the number series, then $m = k$. To do this suppose there are concepts $F(x)$ and $G(x)$ such that

$$m = \text{the number of } F\text{s and } k = \text{the number of } G\text{s}$$

and there are objects c and d such that

$F(c)$ and $n =$ the number of Fs which are not c and $n =$ the number of Gs which are not d.

Then

the number of Fs which are not $c =$ the number of Gs which are not d.

So there must be a relation, $R(x,y)$, which is a one–one correspondence between these classes. So put

$$R^*(x,y) \equiv_{df} R(x,y) \text{ or } (x = c \text{ and } y = d).$$

$R^*(x,y)$ will be a one–one correspondence between the Fs and the Gs. Hence these have the same number and $m = k$.

(8) y comes before x in the number series
$\equiv_{df} x$ comes after y in the number series
$\equiv_{df}$ for any concept F, $F(x)$ holds whenever F is such that $F(y)$ and, for every number n, if $F(n)$ then also $F(n + 1)$.

(9) n is a finite number $\equiv_{df} n$ is a natural number $\equiv_{df} n$ comes after 0 in the number series.

Definitions (8) and (9) are crucial to Frege's rebuttal of the Kantian view of arithmetic. Kant held that our understanding of the natural numbers and the basis on which all knowledge of them is founded is the construction in the pure productive imagination of a series whose members we count as we construct it. This is the intuition which Frege's definitions (7) and (8) aim to capture – the natural (or finite) numbers are those which can be reached by starting from 0 and successively adding units. Kantians would also argue that there is a form of inference (numerical induction) which is characteristic of arithmetic and whose validity rests on the founding arithmetic intuition – construction of the number series in imagination. If the natural number series is just the series generated from 0 by the successive addition of units then this is a series which can never be completely given. It is always incomplete. The only basis, therefore, on which an assertion can be made about all possible members of the series, no matter how far it may be extended, an assertion of the form $\forall n \, F(n)$, is a proof that $F(0)$ and that, for any n, if $F(n)$ then $F(n + 1)$, since it is then assured that $0, 1, 2, \ldots, n, n + 1, \ldots$ will each satisfy $F(x)$. This form of inductive inference works for natural numbers, where it does not work for empirical generalizations precisely because the numbers are not empirically given objects, known only through experience, but are objects which we construct in the process of imaginatively generating a series. Their properties are therefore only those which stem from their constructive generation.

Frege, on the other hand, whilst not for a minute wishing to deny that numerical induction is a valid principle of arithmetic reasoning, had to claim that it is not a principle whose validity rests on an intuition of the natural numbers as products of mental construction. His position was that this is in fact a slightly disguised logical principle. Once the correct definitions have been given, it can in fact be shown to be simply a matter of applying the definition of what it is to be a natural number, combined with the definition which explains what it is for one object to come after another in an R-series, i.e. a series where each member stands in some fixed relation R to the one which immediately precedes it (in the case of the natural numbers the relation in question is $n = m + 1$). Frege did not see an R-series as something which is generated or constructed. The objects (including numbers) already exist and it is a determinate matter which of them do or do not stand in the relation R to one another. It is therefore also a

determinate matter as to whether one object follows another in the
R-series or not.

§80 . . . Whether y follows in the f-series after x has in general
absolutely nothing to do with our attention and the circumstances in which we transfer it; on the contrary, it is a
question of fact, just as much as it is a fact that a green leaf
reflects light rays of certain wavelengths whether or not these
fall into my eye and give rise to a sensation, and a fact that a
grain of salt is soluble in water whether or not I drop it into
water and observe the result, and a further fact that it
remains still soluble even when it is utterly impossible for me
to make any experiment with it.

My definition lifts the matter onto a new plane; it is no
longer a question of what is subjectively possible but of what
is objectively definite . . .

Only by means of this definition of following in a series is it
possible to reduce the argument from n to $(n + 1)$, which on
the face of it is peculiar to mathematics, to the general laws
of logic.

(Frege 1950 p. 93)

What now remains to be proved is that for every natural number
there is a number which immediately follows it. The idea behind
the proof that this is the case is that for any natural number n there
will be $n + 1$ natural numbers less than or equal to n.

$$\underbrace{0, 1, 2, 3, \ldots, n}_{n + 1}$$

$n + 1$ will then be the class of classes X for which there is a
one–one correspondence between X and the natural numbers less
than or equal to n. What has to be proved then is that the
definitions given really do have the consequence that for any
natural number n, the number of the class of natural numbers
which either come before n in the number series or are equal to n
does follow immediately after n in the number series.

Clearly, since 1 = the number of objects x such that $0 = x$
and $0 = $ the number of objects y such that $0 = y \ \& \ 0 \neq y$,
1 comes immediately after 0.

Suppose that the number of the classes of natural numbers
which either come before n in the number series or are equal

to n follows immediately after n in the number series. We now want to show that it follows that the same holds with $n + 1$ in place of n.

The number of numbers which come before $n + 1$ or are equal to $n + 1$ is $(n + 1) + 1$ iff (using (7)) there is a c which comes before n in the number series or is equal to $n + 1$ and such that $n + 1$ is the number of things which come before n in the number series or are equal to $n + 1$ and are not identical with c. (i.e. $\exists c \, (c \leq n + 1 \,\&\, n + 1 =$ the number of objects x such that $x \leq n + 1 \,\&\, x \neq c)$).

$n + 1$ provides the required c, since, by assumption, the number of objects $x \leq n$ is $n + 1$.

Now since the natural numbers are, by definition (9), precisely those numbers x for which $F(x)$ holds if $F(0)$ and if whenever $F(n)$ then $F(n + 1)$, the above is sufficient to show that for every natural number n, the number of the class of natural numbers which are less than or equal to n is $n + 1$. (Note that this is an example of proof by numerical induction reduced to the application of the definition of 'natural number'.)

Thus the definitions are sufficient to establish that there is a natural number following immediately after every natural number. From this it also follows that there are infinitely many natural numbers since for every natural number there is a next in the series and the series never loops back on itself, i.e. no natural number comes after itself in the number series. Intuitively there is a number coming after any given number n because each n itself gives a way of getting to the next number – add n to the number series, to get the series 0, 1, 2, ..., $n - 1$, n and there is an example of a class with $n + 1$ members. That this series never loops back on itself is characteristic of finite numbers but not of numbers generally. Frege's definition allows for the possibility of infinite numbers.

For example, the number of even finite numbers is the same as the number of odd finite numbers and the number of all finite numbers, for each even number can be uniquely paired with an odd number and the function $f(n) = 2n$ pairs each finite number with a unique even number. Yet in spite of this, according to definition (7), the number of the class of even numbers, say E, ought to come before that of the class of all finite numbers in that if we start with the class of even numbers and add an odd number to it

$$0, 2, 4, 6, \ldots, 1$$
$$1, 0, 2, 4, \ldots$$

then we should have something whose number is $E + 1$, yet, as indicated above, there is a one–one correspondence between $E + 1$ and E so that $E + 1 = E$. It is possible to do this because there are infinitely many even numbers, so we shall never run out of them when trying to count both the odd and the even numbers.

This can all be proved formally and logically, as Frege demonstrated, but requires the introduction of the full formal logical apparatus to fill in all the steps. For present purposes it is sufficient to see how Frege's programme was supposed to work and what gives it plausibility, but at the same time one cannot help feeling that there has been some kind of trick; that Frege has just been playing, albeit very cleverly, with words and symbols, but that he hasn't really done anything except show us how to play a new and rather complicated game.

WORD GAMES?

How has Frege made it possible to define the names of numbers in such a way that propositions concerning them become provable from their definitions? Has he not just substituted one game, logic chopping, for the original calculation game? On what basis could he have claimed to have revealed the nature of arithmetical truths? When we go through Frege's definitions we get a sense of a magician pulling rabbits out of a hat; there seems to be some trick. We start literally from nothing and end up with infinitely many numbers. Where do the rabbits, or numbers, come from? They come from the extended powers of definition (mentioned on pp. 45–6) which make what Frege calls 'fruitful' definitions possible. Of these Frege says:

> What we shall be able to infer from it, cannot be inspected in advance; here we are not simply taking out of the box again what we have just put into it. The conclusions we draw from it extend our knowledge, and ought, therefore, on Kant's view, to be regarded as synthetic; and yet they can be proved by purely logical means, and are thus analytic. The truth is

that they are contained in the definition, but as plants are contained in their seeds, not as beams are contained in a house. Often we need several definitions for the proof of some proposition, which consequently is not contained in any one of them alone, yet does follow purely logically from all of them together.

(Frege 1950 p. 101)

Yet extending powers of definition does not in itself yield any reassurance that Frege has not just introduced a new and rather more complicated game where numbers are being constructed by complex verbal routes rather than in pure creative imagination. Frege clearly wished to claim much more than this, for he was highly critical of the formalist attitude toward arithmetic and its extension into real and complex numbers.

For the formalist all that is required to introduce numbers is that symbols be introduced together with rules for manipulating them in calculations in such a way that the resulting system is free from contradiction. So one can define the new symbol 'i' by '$i =_{df} \sqrt{(-1)}$' and extend definitions of addition, subtraction and multiplication to integrate this new symbol into the normal number system. This generates not just one new number, i, but a whole new number system, the complex numbers. Frege was very critical of this attitude.

§96 . . . even the mathematician cannot create things at will, any more than the geographer can; he too can only discover what is there and give it a name.

(Frege 1950 p. 108)

Nonetheless one still has to determine in what way his own procedure really differs from it. In what way are his definitions of the natural numbers supposed to be superior to this kind of formalist definition? An answer to this question is indicated in the following quotation:

§97 . . . Nothing prevents us from using the concept 'square root of -1'; but we are not entitled to put the definite article in front of it without more ado and take the expression 'the square root of -1' as having a sense.

(Frege 1950 p. 106)

A definition, for Frege, has to give sense to the expression being defined; it cannot merely serve to introduce a word or symbol with which to play pencil and paper games. An expression has been given a sense only when its definition serves as a basis for being able to see what is required for the truth or falsity of every sentence in which it could occur. Furthermore, if the definition is introducing an expression which is supposed to be the name of an object, as is the case with '$i =_{df} \sqrt{(-1)}$', it is not adequate unless it can be established that there cannot be more than one square root of -1. For example, 4 has two square roots, $+2$ and -2, so we might well imagine that if negative numbers have square roots at all, they also have two. If there were more than one square root of -1 then the definition of i would not serve as a basis for determining the truth value of sentences in which it might occur, for we would first need to know which of the square roots was being referred to. So in this case the prior problem is to give a sense to the expression '$\sqrt{(-1)}$'.

But how can it be proved that a name, or other expression, has been adequately defined? How is it ensured that an expression has been given a sense? This can only be done if the definition equates the sense of the newly defined expression with that of a combination of previously defined expressions, a combination whose own sense is not in doubt. If we look at Frege's definition

(3)   the number of Fs $=_{df}$ the class of classes X which are equinumerous with the Fs

we have to note how closely it is linked to his original thought that what has to be determined is a sense for statements asserting the identity or non-identity of two numbers and that this is given by

(1)   the number of Fs = the number of Gs iff there is a one–one correspondence between the Fs and the Gs.

It is the sense of 'there is a one–one correspondence between the Fs and the Gs' which is the sense of the identity statement for the corresponding numbers (it is just seen as being put together in a different way – Frege talks here of carving up the content of a sentence in a new way) and it is the understanding of what it is to be a one–one correspondence (something which can be logically expressed) which assures Frege that this is an equivalence relation. This in turn ensures that any class (extension of a concept) will be in just one equivalence class, so underwriting the legitimacy of the definition of 'the number of Fs'. Frege's definitions of the numerals '0', '1', '2', ... are such that they have the consequence that

the number of Fs $= n$ iff there is a one–one correspondence
between the Fs and the natural numbers less than n.

Here one could say that it is this analysis of the use of numbers in
their most basic application (counting, or measuring the size of a
collection of objects) which ultimately supplies sense to the
numerals and to equations, such as '$7 + 5 = 12$'. This sense is
packaged into the definitions in such a way that it can be unpacked
from them again by appeal to logical principles and the definitions.
But the sense has also been repackaged in such a way that it is now
possible to say all sorts of things about numbers, perform operations on them and establish relations between them without ever
thinking about their applications, even though the definitions
make it clear how the results of this abstract reasoning are to be
applied.

§87 ... To apply arithmetic in the physical sciences is to bring
logic to bear on observed facts; calculation becomes deduction. ... The laws of number, therefore, are not really
applicable to external things; they are not laws of nature.
They are, however, applicable to judgements holding good
of things in the external world: they are laws of the laws of
nature. They assert not connections between phenomena,
but connections between judgements; and among judgements are included the laws of nature.

(Frege 1950 p. 99)

These judgements have an objective content, something which
is not a combination of ideas in the mind of an individual, but
something which has an existence independently of individual
minds. The laws of logic, mapping the relations between judgements, are not laws of thought conceived as a psychological
process, but laws of the relations between thoughts conceived as
the contents of (possible) judgements, which do not depend on
there being anyone who is or has entertained them. As such the
laws of logic are themselves objective truths. To say that A is a
logical consequence of B is to say something which is objectively
true or false, quite independently of whether anyone has made the
connection between A and B. We reason correctly when we follow
the pattern of objectively determined consequence relations, and
incorrectly when we do not. Arithmetic like formal logic is simply
one of the ways in which we establish the pattern of connections

between types of judgement; calculation makes it possible to move around the pattern without having to worry about the specific content of the judgements (i.e. whether we happen to be talking about sheep, goats or dollars). The mathematician is then discerning these patterns and providing a language in which to represent them; he cannot create at will but must start from judgements with content and the possible kinds of logical connection between them. He can define concepts but must show them to be free from contradiction before any kind of legitimacy can be claimed.

§95 ... Strictly, of course, we can only establish that a concept is free from contradiction by first producing something that falls under it. The converse inference is a fallacy.
(Frege 1950 p. 106)

If Frege's definitions really did what he claimed they would do, if they really ensured that the names he defined had references, he would thereby also have demonstrated the consistency of arithmetic. Ironically, it turns out that his own system is inconsistent; the attempt to ensure that the definitions of numbers as objects really do secure reference, that they provide a way of in principle determining that every statement about numbers is either true or false, failed.

Where did Frege go wrong? This is not an easy question to answer. He was certainly right about one thing: once the powers of definition are extended by the introduction of relations, the tracing of logical consequences is no longer a simple matter. In pursuit of an even more radical reduction of mathematics to logic than Frege had ever envisioned, Russell discovered an inconsistency in Frege's system. This was in 1902, when the second volume of Frege's *Grundgesetze* was still in press. Russell also proposed a diagnosis of the inconsistency in Frege's logic, which has been widely accepted but which, as we shall see, leaves many of the issues which Frege was addressing essentially unanswered.

3

RUSSELL: MATHEMATICS
AS LOGIC

logic has become more mathematical and mathematics
has become more logical. The consequence is that it has now
become wholly impossible to draw a line between the two; in
fact, the two are one. They differ as boy and man; logic is the
youth of mathematics and mathematics is the manhood of
logic.

(Russell 1919 p. 194)

In his *Principles of Mathematics* (1903) Russell arrived at a view of
arithmetic which was strikingly similar to that of Frege but he
came there by a different route. As he relates, he was initially
concerned with the foundations of dynamics, and was led to
thinking about geometry and thence to numbers and arithmetic via
the work of Cantor (1955) and Peano (1889). Cantor developed a
theory of infinite numbers as part of the general project of
nineteenth century mathematicians to construct a numerical model
of the geometrical continuum (see Tiles 1989). Peano is known
principally for his axiomatization of arithmetic, but the logical
symbolism now familiar through Russell's work was adapted from
Peano. Before writing the *Principles of Mathematics* Russell had
published a shorter book on the foundations of geometry (Russell
1897) in which he subjected the Kantian view of geometry and the
whole idea that there could be synthetic *a priori* truths to searching
scrutiny. His *Principles of Mathematics* is a non-formal and wide
ranging discussion of foundational issues in which he argues, in a
programmatic way, for a logicist position. Most of the book was
written before he had read Frege's work and a brief discussion of
Frege is added as an appendix. The formal completion of the
logicist programme, whose outlines had for the most part been

sketched in the *Principles*, was undertaken in collaboration with Whitehead and became the three-volume *Principia Mathematica* (Whitehead and Russell 1910–13). The philosophical upshot of this mammoth undertaking is presented in a non-formal and very accessible form in Russell's *Introduction to Mathematical Philosophy* (Russell 1919) which, because of its accessibility, has probably been the vehicle through which Russell's logicist view of mathematics has been most widely known. However, its order of presentation does not give many clues as to the route by which Russell arrived at his views, since it starts with a consideration of the natural numbers. This leads to a greater assimilation of his views to those of Frege than is strictly warranted.

GEOMETRY AND RELATIONAL STRUCTURES

Whereas Frege had accepted Kant's views on the synthetic *a priori* status of geometry according to which the axioms of Euclidean geometry are truths grounded in *a priori* intuitions of space and time, Russell did not. Russell's position is derived from his realization of the importance of the discovery of non-Euclidean geometries: the realization that they make the question of what exactly is the correct geometrical description of physical space a non-trivial question. Euclidean geometry can no longer be regarded as automatically applicable to physical space once it is realized that alternative geometries are possible and that their properties can be mathematically investigated. Russell was impressed by the results obtained in projective geometry and suggested that, since the axioms of projective geometry are common to Euclidean and non-Euclidean geometries, they are known *a priori* whereas the axioms which determine the specific metric geometry of space can be known only *a posteriori*. In his *Foundations of Geometry* Russell argues, contra Kant, that it is not Euclidean space which is a necessary condition of experience but a 'form of externality' which ensures that experience takes the form of simultaneously presented but distinct things. In our actual world this form is provided by space. This, however, is a contingent matter; that it is space which provides the form of externality is known only *a posteriori*, through sense perception. Thus it is only through sense perception that the character of space can be known (Russell 1897 p. 186). If the axioms of Euclidean geometry are not *a priori* truths about physical space then the question of what exactly it is that geometers have been and continue to be engaged in studying must naturally arise. Russell's initial and fairly simplistic view of geometry is that the mathematician merely establishes what are the consequences of the axioms of a particular geometry. His knowledge then takes the form 'If axioms $A_1 \ldots A_n$ are true in space S, then . . .'. There may or may not exist a space of which the particular axioms are true, but this is not the mathematician's concern; it is for the physicist to determine what is the likely geometry of physical space, or space–time. Knowledge of the character of physical space, or space–time, will be gained empirically so that if it is possible at all it will be synthetic *a posteriori* knowledge.

However, separating the mathematical study of geometry from the empirical study of physical space in this way does not yet establish that the mathematical study reduces to logic. To claim that geometrical knowledge is no more than knowledge of logical consequences of definitions it has to be shown that conditional statements of the form 'If the axioms $A_1 \ldots A_n$ of geometry G are true in space S then . . .' can be established by logical deduction. I.e. geometrical theorems must be purely logical consequences of their axioms and deductions must not rely on any appeals to geometrical intuition. If we think of geometry as presented in the tradition of Euclid, this is far from obvious. One needs to bring to his axioms some intuitive understanding of the terms 'point' and 'line' in order to derive any consequences from them. An intuitive grasp of these concepts is also necessary if one is to understand Euclid's definitions of geometrical figures such as the circle and the triangle. (See for example the simple proof given at the beginning of Chapter 1.) Moreover, to be assured of the consistency of the axioms of a geometry it would seem that one needs some sort of intuition of a space in which they are all true. The non-Euclidean geometries in which the axiom of parallels is denied in a variety of ways were only established as possibilities when it was shown that they could be modelled in Euclidean space. For example, the surface of a sphere provides a model of a two-dimensional Riemannian space.

Here straight lines (the shortest distance between any two points) are great circles and consequently two straight lines which would have been parallel, because they are both perpendicular to a given line, and hence would never meet in Euclidean space, will now meet in two places. If the axioms of Euclidean

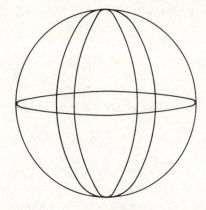

Figure 6

three-dimensional space are consistent, then so are those of Riemannian two-dimensional space. But the assurance we have of the consistency of the Euclidean axioms relies on the intuitive ability to imagine a space in which they are true.

These are essentially the objections which Frege presented to Hilbert (Frege 1971). The basic disagreement, as Frege perceives, is that Hilbert (and Russell)

> wants to divorce geometry completely from our intuition of
> space and make it a purely logical discipline, like arithmetic.
> (Frege 1971 p. 14)

This is precisely the move on which Russell's claim that the whole of mathematics is reducible to logic depends. What Hilbert provided was an axiomatization of Euclidean geometry which takes rigour far beyond anything required by Euclid. Additional axioms are introduced as a result of an analysis of the assumptions about space which were for Frege, as for Euclid, supplied by geometrical intuition. But once these axioms are provided, *any* collection of objects of which they are true will be considered a Euclidean 'space'.

Now there is a sense in which this is merely a way of making explicit what was already implicit in the practice of drawing graphs in which, for example, velocity is plotted against time. This spatial representation presumes that velocities and times form one-dimensional 'spaces' which can be combined to give the two dimensions of a two-dimensional Euclidean 'space'. Hilbert's axiomatization fails to privilege space as ordinarily understood; geometry applies to any collection of entities exhibiting a certain kind of structure and the point of the full axiomatization is to specify exactly what sort of structure is required for a Euclidean as opposed to some other geometry. For example there are seven axioms for the 'betweenness' relation which is characteristic of points on a line, as opposed to those on the circumference of a circle or other closed curve. This means (said Hilbert and Russell) that a line (a,b) can be defined to be the set of points x such that a betweenness relation satisfying the following seven conditions holds between the three points a, b, x in some order or other.

1 If there is an x between a and b then $a \neq b$.
2 If x is between a and b, then x is also between b and a.
3 If x is between a and b, then $x \neq a$.
4 If x is between a and b, then any y between a and x is also between a and b.
5 If x is between a and b, and b is between x and y, then b is between a and y.
6 If x and y are both between a and b, then either $x = y$ or x is between a and y or x is between y and b.
7 If b is between a and x and also between a and y, then either $x = y$ or x is between b and y or y is between b and x.

Intuitively, given any two points a and b the line joining them consists of three parts: (i) the points between a and b, (ii) the points x such that a is between x and b, (iii) the points y such that b is between y and a. If a and b were points on the circumference of a circle, then any other point x on the circumference could be said to be between a and b since one could always get from a to b via x. Indeed x could be said to be between a and a so that condition (1) above would not be satisfied.

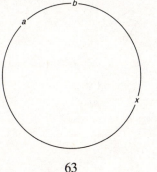

Figure 7

The seven conditions given above merely ensure that the 'points' on a 'line' come in a linear sequence. They do not ensure that the points will be all those that we would normally expect there to be on a line. A geometrical line, for example, is indefinitely divisible, i.e. for any points x and y on the line, if $x \neq y$ then there is a point z such that z is between x and y. Further conditions can be added to give a more complete specification of the sort of structure required of a geometrical line. But what is significant is that formal, logically expressible conditions on a relation can be used to characterize the sort of structure exhibited by any collection of objects over which there is a relation satisfying that set of formally expressed conditions.

To illustrate this further, suppose that there is a relation $R(x,y)$ defined over the collection of objects $a_1 \ldots a_5$ and a relation $S(x,y)$ defined over the collection of objects $b_1 \ldots b_5$. Suppose also that there is a function $f(x)$ mapping each a to exactly one b and such that for every b there is an a such that $b = f(a)$ (i.e. f sets up a one–one correspondence between the as and the bs). Suppose further that f is such that $R(a_i,a_j)$ iff $S(f(a_i),f(a_j))$. In this case f is said to be an *isomorphism* and the as together with R are said to be *isomorphic* to the bs together with S; in other words, they have the same structure, as illustrated below.

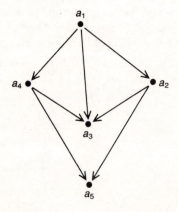

Figure 8

Suppose the following is a complete list of the R-relations between as:

$$R(a_1,a_2), R(a_1,a_3), R(a_1,a_4), R(a_2,a_3), R(a_2,a_5), R(a_4,a_3), R(a_4,a_5)$$

Suppose that f maps $a_1 \mapsto b_5, a_2 \mapsto b_4, a_3 \mapsto b_3, a_4 \mapsto b_2, a_5 \mapsto b_1$. Then the following will be a complete list of the S-relations between the bs, given that f is an isomorphism.

$$S(b_5,b_4), S(b_5,b_3), S(b_5,b_2), S(b_4,b_3), S(b_4,b_1), S(b_2,b_3), S(b_2,b_1)$$

And the structure of the bs under S will have the same pictorial representation as that of the as under R.

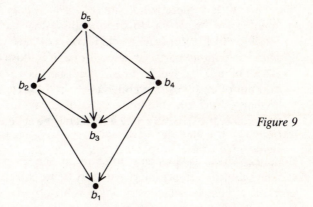

Figure 9

What Russell and Hilbert were reflecting in their remarks on geometry was the extent to which mathematicians themselves had come to focus on structure in a sense which was no longer restricted to spatial or numerical structure but which represented a generalization and abstraction from these. The ability to develop a formal logic of relations was again crucial to the ability to make this move. Once we think of two different sets as exhibiting the same structure, it becomes apparent that the structure does not depend on the particular objects in the set, or even on the specific relations between them, but on the pattern of their relationships. Structures arise out of relations of isomorphism in much the same way that numbers arise out of one–one correspondences. To the extent that structures can be characterized by placing logically formulated conditions on relations, it becomes at least plausible to suggest that the mathematical investigation of structure is an investigation of the logical consequences of sets of axioms.

The idea that the geometers' concern is with structure and not with the specific entities forming the structure is one which played a very central role in Russell's philosophy, a role which extends well beyond the confines of the philosophy of mathematics. He drew the conclusion that

> the mathematician need not concern himself with the particular being or intrinsic nature of his points, lines, and planes, even when he is speculating as an *applied* mathematician. We may say that there is empirical evidence of the approximate truth of such parts of geometry as are not matters of definition. But there is no empirical evidence as to what a 'point' is to be. It has to be something that as nearly as possible satisfies our axioms, but it does not have to be 'very small' or 'without parts'. Whether or not it is those things is a matter of indifference, so long as it satisfies the axioms. If we can, out of empirical material, construct a logical structure, no matter how complicated, which will satisfy our geometrical axioms, the structure may legitimately be called a 'point'.
>
> (Russell 1919 p. 59)

Contained here is Russell's solution to the empiricist's long standing difficulty concerning geometry. The objects of which it purports to give knowledge are not possible objects of perception (sense experience); we could not see or feel a mathematical point or a mathematical line. How then could conceptions of such things, let alone knowledge of their properties, be derived from experience as the empiricist would require if geometry is to be allowed to have any application to the world of experience. Russell's answer is that any entities which can be defined from empirically derived material and which satisfy the geometrical axioms will serve to indicate exactly what sort of application geometry has in the empirical world. They will also serve as the theoretical objects by means of which the geometer discusses geometrical structure. Here there can be no thought of a uniquely correct collection of objects since

> what matters in mathematics, and to a very great extent in physical science, is not the intrinsic nature of our terms, but the logical nature of their inter-relations.
>
> (Russell 1919 p. 59)

Russell expands on this slightly cryptic remark a couple of pages later, where he uses this idea to support his view of what can be the content of statements giving objective knowledge of the physical world. Russell takes it that the physical world does exist independently of our perception of it, that our perceptions (or sensations), are caused by constituents of this physical world (sense data) and that the causal relation is such that different perceptions must have proceeded from causes which are different from one another. In other words, if we pay attention only to the relations of similarity and difference between perceptions we shall be justified in assuming the pattern of these relations (the structure) to be isomorphic to the pattern of relations of similarity and difference obtaining between their causes (an idea he might well have borrowed from Leibniz).

> If the phenomenal world has three dimensions, so must the world behind phenomena; if the phenomenal world is Euclidean, so must the other be; and so on. In short, every proposition having a communicable significance must be true of both worlds or of neither: the only difference must lie in just the essence of individuality which always eludes words and baffles description, but which, for that very reason, is irrelevant to science.
>
> (Russell 1919 p. 61)

Indeed, since the qualities of a sensation can be known only to the perceiving subject and are dependent on his perceptual apparatus, these cannot be any part of what can be communicated about the world assumed to be common to and to exist independently of perceiving subjects. Russell was as insistent as Frege on excluding any psychological contribution to the content of objective knowledge although, as his very different treatment of geometry illustrates, the two philosophers end up with very different views of the possible content of objective knowledge of the physical world. For Russell objective knowledge of the physical world can only concern the structure of relations between items of possible experience. Mathematics is especially suitable for expressing these relations since the process of measurement itself involves comparison between objects – the measuring apparatus and the thing measured.

Here Russell makes implicit assumptions about the world of experience and about the physical world which gives rise to this experience. He makes these assumptions explicit in the Preface to the *Principles* (Russell 1903 p. xviii). They are that the world is made up of mutually independent entities between which there are ultimate, non-reducible relations, i.e. relations which are external relations. (This is the position for which, in the *Foundations of Geometry*, he had presented a transcendental argument but which he now presents merely as a necessary assumption.) If *R* is an external relation between *a* and *b* it is not possible to deduce whether *Rab* is true or false from knowledge of the properties of *a* and *b* or from knowledge of any larger whole which they may form. In other words, if true *Rab* would be a contingent truth knowable only *a posteriori*. This is very much the character of the world of experience (a sequence of impressions) inhabited by Hume, who claimed that each impression is a distinct and independent existent. The spatial or temporal relations in which Humean impressions stand to one another are external relations; the same impressions might have occurred in a different sequence and similar impressions might well occur in a different sequence in the future (hence the deductively ungrounded character of predictions of the future based on past experience). This morning the train might have left the station before I reached it, although in fact it did not. For Hume, however, relations of similarity and difference between impressions, such as similarity of colour, would be internal relations based on the qualities of the individual impressions and are counted among the relations of ideas. An impression of leaf-textured green could not be the impression it is and have a different colour (it could not have been that impression and have been of purple) so it necessarily stands in a relation of colour similarity to an impression of grass-textured green. But Russell is not counting qualities, such as colour, as objectively communicable. So for him it will be a contingent matter that the sensation caused by whatever it is that I am looking at when I see grass is similar in colour to the sensation caused by whatever it is that I am looking at when I see a tree. The relation of similarity or difference will be irreducible and external because it is being referred to an external world.

Here there is a striking difference between the assumptions made by Russell and by Frege, a difference which carries over onto their accounts of arithmetic and of mathematics more generally. Frege insisted that numbers apply to concepts – we always talk of the number of *F*s, the number of things falling under the concept *F*, because it is only the concept which tells us how to start counting. There is no 'natural' or empirically 'given' unit. Whether presented with the page of a book or the top of a desk, it is impossible to say how many objects are present. We have to know whether to count letters, words, lines, paragraphs, books, sheets of paper, staples ... . The individuation of the world of experience into objects is dependent on its conceptualization, so it cannot be thought to be in itself, without reference to any concepts, simply made up of objects. Frege's way of introducing numbers as objects is consistent with this attitude. What we basically have to know is how to count numbers – when we have the same one again and when a different one. The definitions have the effect of reorganizing the content of one judgement – the existence of a one–one correspondence between the *F*s and the *G*s, into a judgement of identity between numbers. This is merely one instance of the general dependence of objects on criteria of identity, contained in concepts. Identity may be a logical notion but Frege does not presume that there are any primitive, given objects. In this his position is not atomistic.

By contrast Russell's position came to be known as logical atomism. He assumes that there are basic individuals, and hence that there are basic, logically primitive propositions – those asserting that a given relation holds between atomic individuals. This position was more clearly stated by Russell after his contact with Wittgenstein although the outlines were present in his earlier work. (There is a striking similarity between Wittgenstein's *Tractatus* notions of logico-pictorial form and logical space and Russell's remarks about relations and structure (Wittgenstein 1922, remarks numbered 2 ...).) Russell's logical atomism and his philosophy of mathematics came to have a mutually reinforcing character. In the *Principles* he suggested (p. xviii) that this atomism was a necessary condition of his being able to arrive at 'a tolerably satisfactory philosophy of mathematics'. The philosophy of mathematics then created a logico-mathematical framework for articulating the logical atomist vision. The reason why atomism was important for Russell's philosophy of mathematics is that it provided him with a philosophic basis for developing his theories of logical types and hence a means of avoiding the inconsistency encountered in Frege's system.

PARADOXES AND LOGICAL TYPES

The contradiction in Frege's system arises as follows. Since classes, or the extensions of concepts, are objects, and every concept $F(x)$ is such that, for any object a, $F(a)$ is either true or false, it is possible to define the concept 'is a class which belongs to itself':

y is a class which belongs to itself $\equiv_{df}$ there is a concept $F(x)$ such that y is the extension of $F(x)$ and $F(y)$.

The following will then also be a well-defined concept:

$R(x) \equiv_{df} x$ is a class which does not belong to itself, i.e. there is a concept $F(y)$ such that x is the extension of $F(y)$ and $\neg F(x)$.

Now does the extension, r, of $R(x)$, belong to itself? That is, is $R(r)$ true or false?

Suppose $R(r)$ is true.
Then r is a class which does not belong to itself, i.e. there is a concept $F(x)$ such that r is the extension of $F(x)$ and $\neg F(r)$.
Suppose that r is the extension of $F(x)$ and $\neg F(r)$. Then since r is also the extension of $R(x)$, the extension of $R(x)$ = the extension of $F(x)$, i.e. $\forall x\, (F(x) \equiv G(x))$.
So, since $\neg F(r)$, $\neg R(r)$ must also be true, i.e. if $R(r)$ is true, $R(r)$ is false – a contradiction.
Suppose $R(r)$ is false.
Then $\neg R(r)$ is true and since r is the extension of $R(x)$, there is a concept $R(x)$ of which r is the extension and for which $\neg R(r)$, i.e. r is a class which does not belong to itself, and so by definition $R(r)$ is true.
So if $R(r)$ is false, $R(r)$ is true, and again we have a contradiction.

Since Frege's system requires that, providing $R(x)$ and r are well defined, $R(r)$ must be either true or false, and since, by the standards of his system, they are well defined, his system is inconsistent.

Where did Frege go wrong? The analysis on which Russell eventually settled was that Frege had allowed for it to be possible for circularities to creep into his definitions. In particular, if the extension of a concept is to be considered to be the sort of thing to which a number can be attached, then it cannot also be allowed to be an object of the same sort as those which might be its members. If a class can possibly belong to itself then a crucial indeterminacy is introduced. For example, Frege had defined the natural number n to be the class of classes X such that there is a one–one correspondence between X and the class of natural numbers $\leq n - 1$. Suppose there were exactly $n-1$ n-membered classes not counting n itself. Then whether n belongs to itself or not depends on whether it belongs to itself. If it does, then it has n members and so is correctly counted as belonging to itself. If it does not, then it has only $n - 1$ members and so is correctly counted as not belonging to itself. In this case there would be no inconsistency, just a total indeterminacy – there could be no basis for giving one answer or the other; either one would do but neither is required.

The intuitive picture on the basis of which it seems reasonable to think that a concept always gives rise to a class of objects with a wholly determinate membership is that where we imagine a given universe of objects and think of the concept as dividing the universe into those things which fall under the concept and those which do not. But if the extension of the concept is allowed to be an object and a member of the universe, then this picture does not apply. (In Figure 10 the class of Fs would have to have two representations – once as a point and once as an area.) If we think of classes as arising out of our classificatory activities, then the intuitive picture is reasonable, but classes would always be classes of previously given objects. We may then take the further step of classifying classes of objects, but again the new classes so formed would not come under this classification. In this way we would generate a hierarchy of objects.

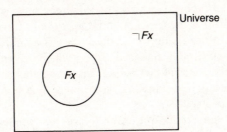

Figure 10

It was by thinking along these lines that Russell was led to introduce what he called the Vicious Circle Principle as an additional logical principle restricting definitions. One formulation of it is as follows:

(VCP) No entity can be defined in terms of a totality of which it is itself a possible member.

This principle gives rise to a hierarchy of kinds of objects (the simple theory of types) and to a corresponding hierarchy of concepts, or propositional functions, as Russell calls them (the Ramified Theory of Types). The Vicious Circle Principle entails that any class, if it is to be allowed to be an object, cannot belong to the totality from which its members are drawn. Thus Russell is led to propose a hierarchy of logical types of objects. The extension of a concept $F(x_0)$ whose argument place can be filled by the name of an individual will be a class of individuals and will thus belong to type 1. If a name for this class were substituted for the individual variable 'x_0' in '$F(x_0)$' the result would be nonsense (a form of words which does not express a proposition and hence has no truth value).

.   .

.   .

.   .

type 2	classes of classes of individuals
type 1	classes of individuals
type 0	individuals

Variables can range only over a single logical type, so concepts can only be defined as applying to objects from a single logical type and all members of a class (the extension of a concept) will all, therefore, always be of the same logical type. This effectively rules out the class which caused trouble for Frege's system. Now no class can possibly belong to itself, and if we were to form a class of classes which do not belong to themselves we should have to specify the type – class of all classes of type 1 which do not belong to themselves. This would in fact be the class of all classes of type 1, and it would itself be a class of type 2 and thus not even a possible member of itself.

Unfortunately the restrictions of even the simple type hierarchy also deprived Russell of some of the appealing aspects of Frege's treatment of arithmetic. Without being able to put together classes from different logical types into a single class it becomes impossible to prove the infinity of the number series. In fact there can no longer be just one sequence of natural numbers if Frege-style definitions are used. If 2 is to be the class of all 2-membered classes the type of the class has to be specified and there will be a whole hierarchy of 2s, one for each type. Moreover, the proof that every natural number has a successor relied upon being able to collect up all the numbers preceding a given number, n, to get a class with $n + 1$ members. This will not work for Russell because a class of numbers is of higher type than any of the numbers of which it is made up and so will not be able to form part of their number series. Russell has to start from individuals and define

$$n =_{df} \text{the class of classes X such that if X is the extension of } F(x_0),$$
$$\text{then } \exists_n F(x_0).$$

If the number of individuals in the universe were finite then for some n we would find that there are no n-membered classes of individuals, i.e. n as defined above would be the empty class (of type 2) as would be $n + 1$ and so on. That is, all numbers greater than n would be the same and there would be only finitely many numbers. Thus to ensure that there are infinitely many numbers Russell has to postulate that there are infinitely many individuals.

From the discussion of geometry in the previous section one might imagine that all this would not matter too much to Russell. His attitude to geometry was that axioms characterize a structure and give all that can be meant by the primitive terms 'point' and 'line'. The mathematician, he said, need not be concerned about the specific identity of the objects to which his theory might be applied. Given this attitude one would not expect him to adopt Frege's approach to arithmetic, an approach which put so much emphasis on defining numbers as objects. One would expect him to favour Peano's route. Peano took the attitude that the primitive terms or arithmetic are '0', 'successor' and 'number' and that the meaning of these is given, as fully as is required or is possible, by the following five axioms of arithmetic.

Peano axioms

1 0 is a number.
2 Every number has a successor which is also a number.
3 No two numbers have the same successor.

4 0 is not the successor of any number.

5 Any property which belongs to 0, and also to the successor of every number which has the property, belongs to all numbers.

It could then be said that any sequence of entities satisfying these axioms is a natural number sequence. Any potentially infinite series in which there is a first term, a successor to every term, no repetitions and every term can be reached from the start in a finite number of steps will satisfy the Peano axioms and hence be a possible natural number sequence. For example:

x_0	x_1	x_2	x_3	
0	2	4	6	...
100	101	102	103	...
1	1/2	1/4	1/8	...

But in fact Russell is critical of this strategy, which he described as having 'all the advantages of theft over honest toil' (Russell 1919 p. 71).

> Such a procedure is not fallacious; indeed for certain purposes it represents a valuable generalization. But from two points of view it fails to give an adequate basis for arithmetic. In the first place, it does not enable us to know whether there are any set of terms verifying Peano's axioms; it does not even give the faintest suggestion of any way of discovering whether there are such sets. In the second place, ... we want our numbers to be such as can be used for counting common objects, and this requires that our numbers should have a *definite* meaning, not merely that they should have certain formal properties. This definite meaning is defined by the logical theory of arithmetic.
>
> (Russell 1919 p. 10)

The first point is precisely similar to the objection which Frege makes to Hilbert's attitude toward the formalization of geometry. The second amounts to endorsing Frege's view of what is required to reduce arithmetic to logic. The argument is that an analysis of the foundations of arithmetic should serve to connect arithmetic, as a mathematical study of numbers with its applications in counting, measuring and calculating.

> This point, that '0' and 'number' and 'successor' cannot be defined by means of Peano's five axioms, but must

be independently understood, is important. We want our numbers not merely to verify mathematical formulae, but to apply in the right way to common objects. We want to have ten fingers and two eyes and one nose. A system in which '1' meant 100, and '2' meant 101, and so on, might be all right for pure mathematics, but would not suit daily life. We want '0' and 'number' and 'successor' to have meaning which will give us the right allowances of fingers and eyes and noses. We have already some knowledge (though not sufficiently articulate or analytic) of what we mean by '1' '2' and so on, and our use of numbers in arithmetic must conform to this knowledge.

(Russell 1919 p. 9)

The task is thus to give definitions of '0', 'number' and 'successor' in such a way that the Peano axioms become logically deducible from those definitions. Numbers are more than a set of entities forming a sequence with a specifiable structure, they are intended as measures. Thus moving up the number sequence and addition of numbers is to be understood in terms of adding things to be counted or measured. For example, one can form an infinite lexical sequence from the alphabet

a b c ... z aa ab ... az ba ... bz ... zz aaa ...

and would in this sense have a sequence satisfying the Peano axioms. But addition of these letters would make no sense unless we start to think of them as numerals, or as standing in for physical magnitudes. It is this further content that has to be given in the definition of '0', 'number' and 'successor'. In particular 0 is to be equated with emptiness, with lack of what it is that is being counted or measured; it is not just the first member in a series but seems required to be a class of empty classes.

But why does Russell think that this should be the case for '0', 'number' and 'successor' and not for 'point' and 'line'? Isn't there an inconsistency here? Even if geometers deal in structures, isn't their primary concern, as Frege argued, with spatial structure? Why, if it would require geometric intuition to supply content to 'point' and 'line', does it not require numerical intuition to supply content to the basic arithmetic notions? If arithmetic reduces to logic is there a founding logical intuition which supplies the content, or does logic somehow generate this content without needing to call upon intuition. One suspects that Russell draws a distinction between the axiomatization of arithmetic and geometry, where Frege does not, because of his empiricist epistemology and its associated metaphysics. He takes it that notions of individual and unit are given in experience (a succession of discrete, individual sensations), whereas the points and lines of geometry are not; they are not possible objects of perception and hence must be some sort of logical construction out of whatever is given. Frege, on the other hand, takes neither units nor points and lines as empirically given.

Being thus committed to adopt the same sort of approach to arithmetic as Frege, Russell cannot avoid having to postulate that there are infinitely many individuals.

Axiom of Infinity There are infinitely many individuals.

He admitted that this postulate, which cannot be dispensed with if he is to have an account of arithmetic satisfying his constraints, cannot be considered to be a logical truth, but is a contingent empirical claim (Russell 1919 p. 141). Note that if intuitions of space and time were allowed, then their continuity, as a result of which they are indefinitely divisible, would already give an infinity of regions of space or periods of time. But Russell has denied the possibility of such *a priori* intuitions and insists that such knowledge of space and time as can be gleaned from experience does not, and cannot, suffice to establish their continuity. Moreover this is not the only postulate that he required.

The simple type hierarchy of objects already introduced an implicit hierarchy of concepts, but the Vicious Circle Principle also put restrictions on the way in which concepts can be defined from relations by using quantification. For example a definition having the form

$$C(x) \equiv_{df} \exists \phi \ (x = \text{the extension of } \phi)$$

which is the form of Frege's definition of 'x is a class', would not be legitimate because $C(x)$ is being defined by quantification over a totality to which it would itself belong. More significantly, Frege's definition of the natural numbers also violates the Vicious Circle Principle. This definition has the form

$$N(x) \equiv_{df} \forall \phi \ (\phi(0) \ \& \ \forall y \ (\phi y \rightarrow \phi(y + 1)) \rightarrow \phi(x)).$$

Here, because the quantification is universal, the circularity is more apparent. Suppose one were to try to determine whether

76

$N(a)$. Then, for each concept $F(x)$ one would need to check to see whether

$$(F(0) \;\&\; \forall y \;(F(y) \to F(y + 1))) \to F(a)$$

and this would include checking to see whether

(N) $(N(0) \;\&\; \forall y \;(N(y) \to N(y + 1))) \to N(a).$

Since $N(0) \;\&\; \forall y \;(N(y) \to N(y + 1))$ will be true by definition, the truth of (N) turns on that of $N(a)$. But this is what was to be determined in the first place. So again, if we are thinking that the definition of a concept $F(x)$ should provide the means for determining the truth or falsity of every statement of the form $F(a)$, then the definition of a concept cannot be allowed to include quantification over a domain to which the concept being defined would belong. This generates yet another and much more complicated hierarchy, whence the name 'Ramified Theory of Types', whose full ramifications need not be investigated here. What is crucial is its bearing on the attempt to define the natural numbers and for these purposes we can simplify somewhat.

The situation is that not only are individuals and classes of individuals different kinds of object, but there is also a stratification within concepts applying to individuals. This stratification is based on how they are defined.

$$
\begin{array}{llll}
& \vdots & \vdots & \vdots \\
& \cdot & \cdot & \cdot \\
\text{concepts of type 3} - F_3(x) & \forall \phi_2\; R_3(\phi_2, x) & \exists \phi_2\; R_3(\phi_2, x) & \dots \\
\text{concepts of type 2} - F_2(x) & \forall \phi_1\; R_2(\phi_1, x) & \exists \phi_1\; R_2(\phi_1, x) & \dots \\
\text{concepts of type 1} - F_1(x) & \forall y\; R_1(x, y) & \exists y\; R_1(x, y) & \dots \\
\text{individuals} & \; x \quad\quad\; a\, b \dots
\end{array}
$$

The extensions of all of these concepts would be classes of individuals. But there is no way to talk about all the concepts which could apply to individuals since the hierarchy is potentially infinite and quantifiers can only range over one type at a time. Yet if the reduction of arithmetic to logic is to succeed, Russell had to define the natural numbers in such a way that the principle of numerical induction reduces to a logical procedure. To make this possible Russell has to introduce a second postulate.

Axiom of Reducibility

For every concept $F_i(x)$ of objects of type n, for $i > n$, there exists an extensionally equivalent concept $G_{n+1}(x)$ of type $n + 1$, i.e. a concept $G_{n+1}(x)$ such that $\forall x\ G_{n+1}(x) \equiv F_i(x)$.

This axiom asserts that increasingly complex definitions do not give any new powers of classification – all classes of individuals can be marked out with basic concepts of type 1, and all classes of objects of type n can be marked out by concepts of type $n + 1$. This means that when using a version of Frege's definition of 'natural number' but with its quantifier limited to ranging only over concepts whose type is next above that of the numbers being defined one will have achieved almost the same effect as quantifying over all concepts, of whatever type, since one will have quantified over all the classes that they could delimit.

This is again a principle which has to be admitted not to be a purely logical principle. It is not something which can be proved, or even, strictly speaking, formulated as a logically legitimate statement, for it involves generalizing over concepts of more than one type and is thus not itself logically correct. Russell is by this means able to avoid the inconsistencies of Frege's system and retain many of the essentials of his account of arithmetic but only at a price and only in a way which must lead one to ask whether he has not demonstrated that and why arithmetic is not reducible to logic, rather than that it is. To evaluate the position further it is necessary to inquire into Russell's justification for adopting the Vicious Circle Principle.

EMPIRICISM, LOGICAL POSITIVISM AND THE STERILITY OF REASON

If one were to adopt a strongly Platonist position, saying that numbers, classes, concepts and functions have an existence which is independent of us and our mathematical activities, then the Vicious Circle Principle could not be justified as a general logical principle. A definition such as

Ben Cullin $=_{df}$ the highest mountain in the Hebrides

which specifies the reference of a name by quantifying over a class in order to select an individual member from that same class, violates the Vicious Circle Principle. Nonetheless, provided that we are confident that there must be a highest mountain in the Hebrides (there are mountains there, all mountains are comparable with respect to height and it is extremely unlikely that there are two of exactly the same height), the definition would normally be regarded as legitimate, even though it does not necessarily provide sufficient information to enable someone to identify the mountain in question. This definition would be regarded as legitimate because the totality by reference to which the name is defined exists as a determinate collection of objects prior to and independently of the definition. The definition does not introduce a new object to add to the totality in question, but names an already existing member. For the Platonist all definitions of (words referring to) numbers, classes, concepts and functions will be of this kind; they are definitions whose function is to link linguistic expressions with pre-existing entities. So for the Platonist, violation of the Vicious Circle Principle cannot, in and of itself, invalidate a definition. This means that he must look elsewhere for a solution to Russell's paradox. One route available to him is to treat Russell's paradox as proving two truths about classes: (i) no class belongs to itself, and (ii) there is no class of all classes. Alternatively he could treat it as indication of a need to distinguish between classes and sets; mathematicians deal with sets and the nature of the set-theoretic universe is captured by the axioms of set theory whose truth is recognized by set-theoretic intuition. These routes are available, but they represent a departure from the logicist programme. Once appeal to set theoretic intuition is allowed it is not clear why intuition of numbers and geometric intuition should not also be allowed.

Russell's advocacy of logicism and his reasons for thinking the Vicious Circle Principle to be a general logical principle are, on the other hand, both grounded in his empiricism. His early, more rationalist, philosophy gave way to empiricism at the same time that his account of mathematics became more closely tied to formal logic. For empiricists the only reality is the empirical world, the world with which we are acquainted through sense experience. Abstract objects, such as numbers or classes, have no independent existence but must be a product of our linguistic or mental constructions. Since there is no realm of mathematical reality of which to have mathematical intuitions, true mathematical statements, if they can be known to be true independently of experience, must be analytic truths, having their origin in the way in which the abstract objects are constructed. As Russell concurred with Frege's desire to separate sharply between the logical and the psychological, he too shied away from any appeal to mental constructions. The objectivity of mathematics requires that the meaning of mathematical language cannot be given by reference to ideas or mental constructions. Rather the meaning of all expressions which apparently refer to abstract objects must be shown, by the provision of suitable definitions, to be logical constructs (fictions) built up from constituents of the empirical world. The assignment of meaning to names can then take one of two forms. Either the name is simply a label for an empirically given object, in which case Russell called it a logically proper name, one which has a reference but no sense, or it is a descriptive expression (a definite description), which identifies an object via its relations to other given objects, or via its mode of construction out of given objects.

The only kind of definition which can be provided for a logically proper name is an ostensive one – the label is attached by pointing to the object and uttering the name. Thus only empirically given entities can have logically proper names. Here Russell disregards Frege's injunction to treat a name as having meaning only in the context of a sentence; logically proper names can function in isolation. Definite descriptions, on the other hand, are always defined in a sentential context. Such expressions are required either for picking out empirical individuals via their relation to other empirical individuals, or for showing how new entities can be constructed out of those which are empirically given or have previously been defined. In the former case one will be using a description to pick out an object from a given class, but in the latter one will not be picking out an already existing entity since one will be introducing a logical fiction. The two cases need to be treated differently if the Vicious Circle Principle is not to seem unduly and unjustifiably restrictive.

Definite descriptions are treated as having meaning only in the context of a sentence. According to Russell's theory of definite descriptions

> Ben Cullin is the highest mountain in the Hebrides $\equiv_{df}$
> There is a highest mountain in the Hebrides, there is at most one and it is Ben Cullin.

Here there is quantification over the domain to which the descriptively identified object belongs, but the definition makes it quite clear that the function of the descriptive phrase is to pick out an object from that domain and that no object is being added to it. Moreover, the descriptive phrase does not have to have a reference for the sentence containing it to make sense. The sentence is simply false if the descriptive identification fails.

Logical fictions are constructed by collecting already defined objects into classes which are themselves regarded as mere fictions. To this end Russell gives contextual definitions showing how apparent reference to classes can be eliminated. For example, the simplest eliminations would be

1 a belongs to the class of Fs $\equiv_{df} F(a)$.
2 the class of Fs = the class of Gs $\equiv_{df} \forall x \, (F(x) \Leftrightarrow G(x))$.

In (2) the Vicious Circle Principle requires that the domain of quantification on the right hand side not include the class of Fs or of Gs. Moreover, it requires that the concepts $F(x)$ and $G(x)$ not themselves contain any quantification over a domain which includes themselves or a domain which includes entities of higher type than their arguments. This means that the actual contextual definitions used in *Principia* have to be somewhat more complicated. The basic idea behind the remaining clauses, which cover the cases where one wants to say things about classes or to form classes into further classes, is that every statement about a class is really a statement about its members (since by (1) and (2) classes are identical when they have the same members). If this is so, then an apparently simple statement about a class can, in principle, be written as a logically complex statement concerning its members. So, for example,

'n = the number of Fs' becomes
'the class of Fs belongs to the class of all n-membered classes'
which in turn reduces to
'$\exists_n xF(x)$'.

It is this view of classes as in principle eliminable logical constructs which justifies the Vicious Circle Principle. An entity (whether object or concept) cannot be constructed out of itself, but only out of entities previously given or constructed. Similarly a verbal expression cannot be defined in terms of itself, but only from expressions which are given as primitive or have previously been defined.

But if this is the justification for the Vicious Circle Principle, then the introduction of the Axiom of Reducibility looks even more embarrassing than it seemed at first sight. Not only is it a non-logical assumption needed for the derivation of arithmetic, and hence an admission of failure in the logicist programme, but, being an existential axiom, it suggests a return to some form of Platonism. This would undercut the Vicious Circle Principle which formed the foundation of Russell's theories of logical types which in turn represented his solution to the paradoxes. This is essentially the argument presented by Gödel (1944). If we are entitled to assume the existence of concepts independently of their definition, as the Axiom of Reducibility seems to assert, then, as outlined above, there is no good reason for thinking the Vicious Circle Principle to be a general logical principle. However, it is also possible to read the Axiom of Reducibility as an assertion of faith in the logicist programme in mathematics, and more generally of the philosophical position of the logical positivists. This does not wholly exonerate Russell. There is a curious circularity in having the success of a position rest on an assertion to the effect that it can be successfully carried out. But, in the first place, it is not clear that any philosophy can ever avoid this kind of circularity and, in the second, it will at least defend Russell against the charge of having introduced an element which renders his position philosophically incoherent.

The position of the logical positivists, unlike that of some earlier empiricists, such as Berkeley and Hume, is not phenomenalist. The logical positivists had, as Russell (1919 p. 170) said, 'a robust sense of reality', i.e. a belief that the empirical world exists independently of us and our experiences – we do not live only in a world of ideas. There is a sharp distinction to be drawn between Hamlet and Napoleon, between unicorns and lions. The former are fictions, existing only as ideas, whereas the latter are empirically real and have an existence beyond our ideas. In this respect their position has more in common with Locke's empiricism than with Hume's. Sense experience affords genuine knowledge of the empirical world and is our only route to knowledge of it. Since this is the only reality of which we have any experience, empirical reality is the only reality which we have any basis for supposing to exist independently of us. (For further discussion and detailed arguments concerning the grounds for belief in the existence of an external world see, for example, Russell (1912).) The only objective knowledge there can be is factual knowledge of this independently existing reality. Since numbers, widthless lines and other mathematical objects are not part of this reality (they are not accessible to sense experience), statements concerning them cannot really embody knowledge of empirical reality but only of relations between the linguistic devices we introduce in order to help us express knowledge of the world efficiently and facilitate reasoning about it. Mathematical truths must thus be a species of logical or analytic truths and these in turn must be products of linguistic conventions. The introduction of mathematical terminology and its use in empirical science must, however, be in principle eliminable. It is a convenience only, one which in principle, if not in practice, could be dispensed with. The same things could be said, the same factual knowledge expressed, without the use of mathematics or any other abstract terminology. (In technical terms, the introduction of mathematical terminology should represent a conservative extension of the language used to talk directly about the empirical world. The case for this position is argued in Field (1980).) But if this is so, and if the world of empirically given individuals and relations between them forms the bottom level of Russellian hierarchies, then it should indeed be the case that concepts definable higher up the hierarchy which have application at the lowest level should not introduce new classifications, since the higher levels should not allow us to say things which couldn't already be said at the lowest level. In other words, the Axiom of Reducibility can be seen as an expression of the belief that all discourse involving expressions for abstract objects which has any empirical content (expresses any genuine knowledge) could be re-expressed in (reduced to) language which does not contain these expressions.

Here the contrast between Frege and Russell on the nature of logic is sharply revealed. Frege's introduction of numbers and other abstract objects through equivalence relations, using definitions of the form

the *** of a = the *** of b $\equiv_{df} R(a,b)$

or of classes via the clause

the class of Fs = the class of Gs $\equiv_{df} \forall x\ (F(x) \Leftrightarrow G(x))$

was taken by Russell, in his later, empiricist period, as an example of how talk apparently about abstract objects is just in fact a way of talking about non-abstract objects. It makes life easier because it facilitates the formulation of generalizations about all objects similar in a given respect. Use of contextual definitions in the theory of definite descriptions and in order to eliminate reference to classes, together with the use of classes to treat abstract objects as logical constructs, formed the basis of the logical positivists' optimism that the new formal logic would be the tool which would make it possible to demonstrate rigorously that and how scientific discourse, employing mathematical and other theoretical terms, serves to represent the empirical world, the world known through sense experience. Where Frege took contextual definitions of names as revealing the identity of genuine independently existing objects, Russell saw them as means of introducing logical fictions (constructs which owe their unity to the logical structure of the definition by which expressions referring to them are introduced). Moreover they are ways of introducing constructs which show that it is not necessary to postulate the existence of constructs. The construction takes place only at the level of language, not in any language-independent world. Thus where Frege saw contextual definition as an indication of the power and fertility of reason, Russell saw it as a procedure by means of which to demonstrate its sterility.

Which of these views can be sustained depends on whether the definitions significantly extend our cognitive powers, our ability to express claims and justify them. Russell's position depends on the correctness of the Axiom of Reducibility. Introducing higher levels of abstraction should make it easier for us to formulate and justify our claims about the empirical world, but not make it possible for us to formulate or justify any claim that could not be made, albeit at greater (possibly infinite) length, without these higher levels. Frege's position rests on his willingness to regard numbers as objects in their own right; justification in no way requires appeal to empirical data. In Frege's hands the definitions introducing numbers clearly do extend the claims it is possible to justify – he can prove the existence of infinitely many numbers. In Russell's hands, given the implementation of the Vicious Circle Principle and type hierarchies, the same definitions do not make it possible to prove this. Instead the infinity of the numbers is contingent upon the existence of infinitely many empirical individuals (something which cannot be proved). Frege's numbers are included in the single domain of objects over which individual variables range. The ability to identify and name new objects thus extends our power of making justified existential claims about this domain. Impredicative definitions can in this way extend our cognitive powers but their legitimacy rests on an assumption of the independent existence of the field of entities for which terminology is being defined. Predicative definitions should not, in principle, extend our cognitive powers, but insistence on a restriction to predicative definitions (those sanctioned by the Vicious Circle Principle) presumes that the entities defined have no existence independent of the constructive procedure indicated in the definition. Gödel made the character of the limitations which would be imposed by this restriction much more explicit in his work on the universe of constructible sets. This universe is constructed by admitting only predicatively definable sets (although it does presume that the infinite ordinal numbers are independently available). Yet the majority of mathematicians agree that this universe is much too small for their purposes. Moreover, restriction to the constructible universe would lead to conflict with accepted results in other areas of mathematics, such as analysis. (For a more detailed discussion of this see Tiles (1989), Chapters 8 and 9.)

Science aims to capture the structure of the empirical world with its laws, and Russell claimed that this structure, although represented mathematically, could be coded into logical structure as a result of the reduction of mathematics to logic. For Russell the point about logical structure is that it is a structure merely displaying the pattern of truth value dependences between propositions. But for him, as for the early Wittgenstein and other empiricists taking their cues from Hume, there can be no such dependences between the basic units of experience, the basic empirical facts. If each impression is a distinct and independent existent, then the truth or falsity of any statement conveying the factual content of such an impression and no more, must be independent of any other such statement. Patterns of truth value dependence are the vehicle for expressing contingent hypotheses concerning the structure of experience. These can directly use quantification over empirically given objects, or employ defined terms where quantification is part of the contextual definition of sentences in which the defined term is used. In either case 'For all x, $F(x)$' is construed as the long conjunction '$F(a)$ & $F(b)$ & $F(c)$ & ...' with $a, b, c, ...$ being a list of all objects in the domain. The position is atomist in that it accords reality only to empirical objects and their relations, not to structure. Structure is pattern arising from and reducible to relations between objects. Here the structural characteristics of basic relations, such as spatio-temporal relations, is also regarded as being a contingent, empirical matter.

For logic to be the inferential framework of objective, factual knowledge, logical structure must be no more than wholly eliminable packaging for empirical content. It cannot be creative whilst providing the vehicle for expression of an objective, undistorted representation of empirical reality. Reason is required, in the interests of factual accuracy, to be sterile. Use of mathematics in science cannot be legitimate if it leads to the imposition of structure which cannot be empirically grounded. We have to guard against mathematical artefacts just as much as against artefacts of the methods of slide preparation when working with a microscope. Russell's ambition was to show that in the case of mathematics one need not be unduly concerned about the risk because mathematics has no structure of its own to impose. Its structures are all logical structures and logic, if its principles are properly formulated, allows form and content to be sharply separated. Its forms do not infect or distort empirical content.

> we should arrive at a language in which everything formal belonged to syntax and not to vocabulary. In such a language we could express *all* the propositions of mathematics even if we did not know one single word of the language. The language of mathematical logic, if it were perfected, would be such a language. . . . It is one of the marks of a proposition of logic that, given a suitable language, such a proposition can be asserted in such a language by a person who knows the syntax without knowing a single word of the vocabulary.
>
> (Russell 1919 p. 213)

Frege did not have an empiricist axe to grind. On the contrary, his goal was to show that logic can be involved with content without having to rely on intuition. Numbers, as logical objects, are objects nonetheless, even though proofs of arithmetical statements need make no appeal to intuitions of these objects. But Frege's system was inconsistent and a logic which is inconsistent does not serve its purpose. Frege despaired of patching his framework and hence of completing his original programme. In his late writings (Frege 1924–5) he reversed his position and returned to the idea that a geometrical intuition is essential even for arithmetic. Frege strongly resisted the reduction of universally quantified statements to long conjunctions of their instances.

> We must not think I mean to assert something about an African chieftain from darkest Africa who is wholly unknown to me, when I say 'all men are mortal'. I am not saying anything about either this man or that man, but I am subordinating the concept man to the concept of what is mortal. . . . What is being spoken about here is a concept, not an individual thing.
>
> (Frege 1979 p. 213)

Where Russell viewed logic as centred on logical truths, Frege is more concerned with logic as embodying principles of inference and like Aristotle he allows that we may learn from inferences and from the fact that certain inferences can be made (see p. 21). The connection between a universal statement such as 'All men are mortal' and the instance 'Plato is mortal' is inferential; it is a matter of inference from general to particular. But he denies that the sense of the particular statement is already contained in that of the general statement. This means that Frege could not regard the conditional statement 'If all men are mortal, then Plato is mortal' as a tautology in Russell's sense. The conditional is a logical truth because it embodies a truth preserving principle of inference. For Russell the direction of justification goes the other way round. The inference from general to particular is logically justified because the conditional statement is a tautology, where the consequent is already one of the propositions forming part of the conjunction which constitutes the antecedent. Here we have contrasting views of the nature of logic and hence of what logicism as a philosophy of mathematics entails. Frege was concerned with arithmetical reasoning and with justifying the claim that neither in pure arithmetic nor in its applications is there any need to call upon principles which would require an appeal to intuition. There are no specifically arithmetic principles involved and thus arithmetic reasoning is just logical deduction; its principles of inference are all universally applicable logical principles. Russell's concern was much more with showing that mathematics does not consist of a body of non-empirical knowledge. If mathematical truths are all logical truths and logical truths are all tautologies – propositions which are true in virtue of their logical form alone, independently of the content of the words they contain – then mathematical truths cannot express *knowledge* of any subject matter.

Russell avoided Frege's inconsistency but the price of consistency is acquiescence in the demands that form and content be sharply separated and that impredicative definition be ruled out. Part of the strength of Frege's position was that he thought he could prove the existence of the infinitely many natural numbers and hence prove the consistency of arithmetic by showing that there is a collection of objects of which the Peano axioms hold. His objection to the formalists, who said that formal consistency was sufficient ground for claiming the existence of mathematical entities, was that proof of the formal consistency of a set of axioms in fact requires provision of a domain in which those axioms can all be shown to hold. How is it possible to know that a set of axioms forms a consistent system without showing that there is a domain of entities of which they are true? One may hope that the system of *Principia Mathematica* is consistent, but how could one demonstrate that this was the case? Russell and Whitehead certainly did not provide such a demonstration. Hilbert thought he had a strategy for responding to Frege's challenge, one which could also be applied to the system of *Principia Mathematica*. Gödel, however, subsequently showed, with his incompleteness theorems, that this strategy cannot be carried out in such a way as to vindicate either the radical logicism of Russell or the formalism derived from Hilbert's Programme.

4

HILBERT: MATHEMATICS AS A FORMULA-GAME?

in my theory contentual inference is replaced by manipulation of signs according to rules; in this way the axiomatic method attains that reliability and perfection that it can and must reach if it is to become the basic instrument of all theoretical research.

(Hilbert 1927 p. 467)

Hilbert was a giant among mathematicians. It is hard to overestimate his influence over the character of twentieth century mathematics; so many of the great names in mathematics studied under him or worked with him in Göttingen. Modern standards of mathematical rigour owe more to Hilbert than to either Frege or Russell, both of whom exerted more influence on philosophy than on mathematics. Hilbert's position was, in a sense, the inverse of Frege's. With his axiomatization of geometry he effectively removed the impulse to treat these axioms as self-evident truths validated by appeal to geometric intuition, or to an intuition of space, for, as he emphasized by saying 'It must be possible to replace in all geometric statements the words *point, line, plane* by *table, chair, mug*' (quoted in Weyl 1970 p. 264) there is nothing peculiarly spatial in the conditions laid down by these axioms; they might be satisfied in any domain of objects. Indeed Frege wrote to Hilbert 'It seems to me that you want to divorce geometry completely from our intuition of space and make it a purely logical discipline, like arithmetic' (Frege 1971 p. 14). Yet Hilbert would not agree with Frege's assumption that arithmetic is a purely logical discipline. He did not think that arithmetic could be reduced to logic or to anything more fundamental. The truths of finitary arithmetic are grounded in an intuitive grasp of notions of unit and of discrete succession as exemplified in the writing of the numerals.

FORMALISM AND HILBERT'S PROGRAMME

Hilbert's 'Programme' was to vindicate classical mathematics, including Cantor's transfinite set theory, by (i) expressing that mathematics in a formal language which could then itself be regarded as an object of mathematical study (in proof theory, or meta-mathematics), and (ii) using only finitary methods to prove that this formal system of infinitary mathematics is consistent by proving that no formula of the form '0 = 1' is provable in it. It is (ii) which Gödel showed to be impossible. Even so the pursuit of Hilbert's goal established new branches of mathematics (proof theory, model theory, recursive function theory) and new ways of thinking about logic, language and reason, for it should be stressed that the conception of (formal) logic to emerge from Hilbert's work is very significantly different from that embraced by Frege and Russell. This difference is important because it tends to be forgotten and thus to be a source of a certain amount of talk at cross purposes between mathematicians and philosophers or, for that matter, between philosophers. Philosophers, to the extent that they have associated logic with the study of language and meaning, have tended to follow in the tradition of Frege and Russell, whereas mathematicians follow Hilbert. It is in Hilbert's work that we find the basis for a fully automated, formal, symbol manipulating reason, reason which can be computer implemented. Yet, paradoxically, this move was made in the cause of defending the free creative power of mathematicians and hence also of reason as embodied in mathematics. 'The goal of my theory is to establish once and for all the certitude of mathematical methods . . . the definitive clarification of the infinite has become necessary, not merely for the special interests of the individual sciences but for the honour of human understanding itself' (Hilbert 1925 pp. 184–5). For this reason Hilbert's position remains attractive to working mathematicians long after Gödel's incompleteness theorems pronounced his full programme to be dead.

Philosophically Hilbert's name is firmly associated with formalism, i.e. with the view that mathematics is essentially a pencil and paper game played with written symbols, a game which can be found useful on occasion but which needs no justification from those applications or from any other source. Since the moves in such a game are neither assertions nor knowledge claims, philosophical questions about the status of mathematical knowledge are bypassed. If such a formalist position could be taken with regard to the whole of mathematics, it would put an end to traditional philosophy of mathematics. Frege was keenly aware of this and devoted considerable space (Frege 1884 §92–§102; 1893 vol. II, §86–§137) to refuting such a claim. The most frequently used analogy compares arithmetic to chess, numerals to chessmen, rules for addition and multiplication to rules for playing chess. If making a step in a calculation is analogous to making a move in chess then there is no assertion, no knowledge claim made. But the analogy fails to establish that there is no arithmetical knowledge, for there is theoretical knowledge associated with chess: there is the theory of the game, there are chess problems which have solutions and claims to have found solutions which are objectively correct or incorrect. Similarly then, even if the analogy is accepted, there will be theoretical knowledge of a recognizably mathematical kind associated with the number game. The assimilation of elementary arithmetic to a computing game does not succeed in reducing number theory to a game or in eliminating all recognizably mathematical knowledge.

But Hilbert never espoused this extreme kind of formalism and indeed he was no formalist when it came to the arithmetic of finite numbers. He praised Frege for having recognized the essential properties of the notion of an integer and the significance of inference by mathematical induction, but he does not accept the claim that arithmetic either has been or can be reduced to logic (Hilbert 1904 p. 130). This is because the notions of set and number are already tacitly employed in expositions of the laws of logic. For example to distinguish between relations and concepts one must already discriminate between functions of one and of two variables.

> Kant taught – and it is an integral part of his doctrine – that mathematics treats a subject matter which is given independently of logic. Mathematics, therefore, can never be grounded solely on logic. Consequently, Frege's and Dedekind's attempts to so ground it were doomed to failure.
>
> (Hilbert 1925 p. 192)

Arithmetic itself is founded in sensory intuition and in our capacity to recognize similarities, differences and order amongst written characters. It was Hilbert's opinion that logic and arithmetic are so closely related that they must be developed hand in hand if paradoxes and contradictions are to be avoided.

Hilbert's formalism has roots in his work on geometry, the theory of real numbers and his appreciation of Cantor's transfinite set theory. For him formalism is a means of defending the axiomatic method and the claim that the only constraint on mathematical investigation is consistency; it is by no means a full account of the nature of mathematical activity. So long as new concepts and new entities can be defined without contradiction then the mathematician has a right to claim that such things exist and are legitimate objects of mathematical investigation. But how is consistency established prior to locating a domain of objects in which the defined concepts are instantiated or of which the axioms postulated are true? Hilbert's proof theory was designed to provide techniques for supplying a precise and unequivocal response to this question, the question over which he and Frege disagreed fundamentally. This disagreement is documented in the correspondence between Frege and Hilbert (see Frege 1971) which occurred after the publication, in 1899, of Hilbert's *Foundations of Geometry*. As a result of his exchanges with Frege and in response to the rising popularity of Brouwer's rejection of infinitary methods (see Brouwer 1912), Hilbert was forced into increasingly philosophical clarifications of his position. That which is best known to English speaking philosophers is 'On the Infinite' (Hilbert 1925). Two others which are readily accessible are 'On the Foundations of Logic and Arithmetic' (Hilbert 1904) and 'The Foundations of Mathematics' (Hilbert 1927). By concentrating only on these late articles, however, it is easy to lose sight of the geometrical origins of Hilbert's position and of the significance of the approach to axiomatization which first emerged clearly in his *Foundations of Geometry*. This provides the groundwork which made modern formalist attitudes toward axiomatization possible.

GEOMETRICAL RIGOUR

Hilbert's *Foundations of Geometry* is a deceptively simple and elegant work in which new standards of rigour are implicitly imposed on the axiomatic presentation of theories. There is also a new conception of what it is that an axiom system can hope to capture. The magnitude of the shift is made apparent by Frege's

reaction to Hilbert's work, for Frege remained thoroughly traditional in his conceptions of geometry and of axiomatization. In the
very brief introduction to his *Foundations of Geometry* Hilbert
states that the aim of the work is

> to establish for geometry a *complete*, and *as simple as
> possible*, set of axioms and to deduce from them the most
> important geometric theorems in such a way that the mean-
> ing of the various groups of axioms, as well as the significance
> of the conclusions that can be drawn from the individual
> axioms comes to light.
>
> (Hilbert 1899 p. 2)

He divided his axioms into five groups. Each of the first three
groups aims to characterize the structure of a single relation: I –
incidence, II – order (see p. 63), III – congruence. Group IV
consists just of an axiom of parallels and group V contains two
continuity axioms. So far this would be a project which Frege
could only endorse. However, in presenting the axioms Hilbert
began:

> DEFINITION. Consider three distinct sets of objects. Let
> the objects of the **first** set be called *points* and be denoted by
> A,B,C, ... ; let the objects of the **second** set be called *lines*
> and be denoted by a,b,c, ... ; let the object of the **third** set
> be called *planes* and be denoted by α,β,γ, ... the points and
> lines and planes are called ... the elements of space.
>
> (Hilbert 1899 p. 3)

Here we are not told how to recognize these objects, merely how
to recognize variables ranging over them. This procedure makes it
quite clear that Hilbert was prepared to countenance any three
sets of objects between which there are relations satisfying his
axioms as a 'space'. What it is to be a point, line or plane, in so far
as these are considered to be the objects with which geometry
deals, is given only by the totality of the axioms. ' ... each new
axiom alters the concept. "Point" is always something different in
Euclidean, non-Euclidean, Archimedean, and non-Archimedean
geometry respectively' (Frege 1971 p. 13). When Frege complained that Hilbert had not given proper definitions because he
had not conferred precise references on his terms and that his
'axioms' were not proper axioms because, containing terms with
no reference, they express no thoughts, Hilbert's response was:

But surely it is self-evident that every theory is merely a framework or scheme of concepts together with their necessary relations to one another, and that the basic elements can be constructed as one pleases. If I think of my points as some system or other of things, e.g. the system of love, of law, or of chimney sweeps ... and then conceive of all my axioms as relations between these things, then my theorems, e.g. the Pythagoras one, will hold of these things as well. In other words, each and every theory can always be applied to infinitely many systems of basic elements.

(Frege 1971 p.13)

In other words, Hilbert sees the purpose of an axiomatic theory, including Euclidean geometry, as being to characterize a type of structure, not to express unique truths about some definite object or set of objects.

Hilbert was one of the first to view axiomatization in this light and to impose standards on the presentation of sets of axioms on the presupposition that their function is not the statement of self-evident truths. His explicit requirements are that the axioms be consistent and mutually independent (i.e. that no axiom should be a logical consequence of the remaining axioms). There is implicitly also a requirement of completeness. Hilbert proves the consistency of his axioms for Euclidean geometry in two stages. He first shows that all the axioms other than V.2 (the second continuity axiom) have a model in a field of algebraic numbers and then that all the axioms, including V.2, have a model in the real numbers, going via Cartesian co-ordinate geometry. In this way he has, additionally, shown the independence of axiom V.2 from the remaining axioms. This axiom is one which Hilbert called the Axiom of Line Completeness and it reads as follows:

> V.2 (**Axiom of line completeness**) An extension of a set of points on a line with its order and congruence relations that would preserve the relations existing among the original elements as well as the fundamental properties of line order and congruence that follows from Axioms I–III, and from V.1 is impossible.

(Hilbert 1899 p. 26)

In other words, for a set S to be a set of 'points' on a 'line' S has to be a maximal model of the preceding axioms. This axiom thus presumes that the other axioms are consistent and do have models which is why Hilbert took the consistency proof in two stages.

Hilbert described this completeness axiom as the cornerstone of the entire system of axioms. It is this axiom which is required to prove the existence of limits corresponding to arbitrary divisions of a line, and other properties normally associated with linear continuity. But this axiom also differs in character from the remainder since it mentions them. In this respect it is a higher order axiom which seeks to secure uniqueness for the structure characterized in the axioms. If the axiomatization is consistent, then there is some basis for claiming that it characterizes a single structure (one which may be realized in many different domains of entities), a single object of mathematical enquiry. Other ways of stating the completeness requirement might then be that the axioms be categorical (all models isomorphic) or that they suffice for the decidability of every sentence involving just the primitive terms of the theory. Hilbert hinted at this latter sense of completeness when he said that once a concept has been completely and unequivocally fixed, then, in his opinion, the addition of any axiom whatever is entirely impermissible and illogical (Frege 1971 p. 13). For if a set of axioms were complete in the sense of rendering every sentence of the language in which they are written decidable, then any additional axiom A would be such that either A or its negation was already entailed by the existing axioms. If A were entailed then to add A would be to add a non-independent axiom and if ¬A were already entailed then the addition of A would render the system inconsistent. But at this stage Hilbert did not have in place the formal machinery necessary to make precise, and thus to distinguish, between various senses of completeness.

Independence is shown for other axioms by providing models, frequently algebraic, in which one axioms fails but the remainder are satisfied. Independence is regarded as important because part of the purpose of an axiomatic presentation of a theory is that it should be possible to be quite clear about the suppositions on which any given theorem depends. In this respect Hilbert is preparing the ground for the incorporation of geometry into the much more general and abstract studies of topology, measure theory etc. If his axioms are consistent and mutually independent then the subtraction of one of them, A, leaves a consistent set of axioms completable in a number of different ways incompatible with A. This depleted set of axioms then characterizes a class of mathematical structures in which all theorems of Euclidean geometry which do not depend on A still hold. In this respect the axiomatic method is no longer devoted to the study of a single theory or single structure but to the systematic study of families of theories or structures (groups, Abelian groups, lattices, topoi) and their interrelations. This is an approach which is now taken so much for granted that it is not easy to comprehend its novelty at the time at which Hilbert was writing. Some sense of this and of the way it changed the agenda for both mathematics and its philosophy can be gleaned by looking briefly at Frege's objections to Hilbert's manner of proceeding.

From Frege's point of view Hilbert went wrong right at the beginning with his so-called 'definition' of points lines and planes, which was no definition at all. Definitions should determine both the sense and the reference of the expressions of which they are definitions. They cannot create *ex nihilo*. To treat the whole set of axioms as determining the meanings of 'point', 'line' and 'plane' is to confuse hopelessly definition with assertion. It is to create logical chaos where one should be introducing clarity. Frege argues that Hilbert should express his axioms using higher order quantification to make it clear that he is not defining the primitive terms at all; these are merely being treated as variables. Thus the first axiom

For every two points A and B, there exists a line that contains each of the points A and B.

should be

For every two objects a and b, if $P(a)$ and $P(b)$ then there is a c such that $L(c)$ and c contains a and b.

The conjunction of the suitably rewritten axioms should then be formed. If P, L and S (for plane) are regarded as free variables, what we then have is a definition of a higher order concept, one which can be satisfied by triples of first order concepts. It then becomes clear that Hilbert is not defining the terms 'point', 'line' and 'plane' at all, but is defining a second level concept. And in one sense Hilbert could agree, he is defining a structure, not specific sets of geometric entities. Yet in another he will disagree because his project is to make clear what the understanding of the terms 'point', 'line' and 'plane' is by showing how they are required to interrelate in the structure which we call Euclidean space. Even Frege admitted that not all terms can be defined and he did not think that it is possible to give definitions of the primitive terms in geometry, only explications. Similarly only explications can be given for fundamental logical notions such as concept and object. ('A *function* is *in need of completion, unsaturated* ... Objects stand opposed to functions.... I count as *objects* everything that is not a function ...' (Frege 1953 pp. 34–6). They cannot be defined because for Frege definition is always reductive; to define a term is to define it in terms of something else. So one might say that since Frege and Hilbert agreed about the impossibility of reducing the primitive terms of geometry to anything else, what they disagreed about was the correct way in which to explicate them. Frege wanted to appeal directly to spatial intuition, whereas Hilbert saw rigorous explication as requiring axiomatization. This comes down to having different views of the nature of geometry and its applications. Frege saw geometry as a body of truths about space. Hilbert, in a spirit prompted by the advent of non-Euclidean geometries, put the application of geometry to physical space on the same footing as other applications. Frege's position had the disadvantage of not making clear the status of the application of geometrical methods in, for example, physics where the magnitudes handled geometrically include time, mass, energy, velocity etc. This was one of the motives for Russell's preference for Hilbert's approach; it renders such applications logically justifiable. However, Hilbert's position seems to lack an account of the subject matter of pure geometry. Whether he agreed with Russell in denying pure geometry its own subject matter is a question which will be taken up in chapter 5.

Since Frege regarded the axioms of Euclidean geometry as expressing a *priori* truths about space, it was obvious to him that they are consistent; there could be no point in trying to prove them consistent. What was required was an assurance as to the *truth* of the axioms. From Frege's point of view the issue raised by the emergence of non-Euclidean geometries was simply that of which is the correct geometry; which axioms are true? He himself had little doubt that the Euclidean axioms are genuine axioms, i.e. express truths about space which are in no need of further proof because their truth is self-evident. Since genuine axioms all have to be true, they cannot stand in need of a consistency proof. Hilbert on the other hand claimed that

If the arbitrarily postulated axioms together with all their consequences do not contradict one another, then they are true and the things defined by these axioms exist. For me this is the criterion of truth and existence.

(Hilbert 1971 p. 13)

But what is it that exists and of what are the axioms true if they are only supposed to be defining a type of structure? As Frege complained:

1. A is an intelligent being.
2. A is omnipresent.
3. A is omnipotent.
Suppose that we know that these propositions, together with all their consequences do not contradict one another. Could we infer from this that there exists an omnipotent, omnipresent, intelligent being? I do not see how. Are there any means of proving consistency other than that of exhibiting an object that has all of the properties? (If one has one then one does not need to prove its existence by going via consistency.)

(Frege 1971 p. 20)

Even if completeness renders the structure defined by the axioms unique, if they have any model at all, it does not guarantee the existence of models. The idea of God also includes maximality. It was precisely this feature which was exploited by Descartes and others in their existence proofs – it would be contradictory to suppose that such a being did not exist. If Hilbert intended his existence claim in a Platonistic sense then he was clearly guilty of the same sort of mistake as Descartes – trying to establish the mind-independent existence of something from the existence of a mind-dependent idea of that thing. But in claiming the existence of a structure as a legitimate object of mathematical investigation, is it a Platonist's, mind-independent existence which is being claimed? Reading back elements of Hilbert's later position into his earlier one, it would be fair to surmise that he regarded the existence of the structures defined by consistent axiom systems solely as ideal, as ideas, as human creations, not as independently existing objects. It has been said that Hilbert lacked sympathy for Kant's philosophy (because of his hostility to Brouwer's intuitionism, which self-consciously drew on Kant's philosophy of arithmetic) but he nevertheless begins the *Foundations of Geometry* with the following quotation:

> All human knowledge thus begins with intuitions, proceeds thence to concepts and ends with ideas.
>
> (Kant 1929 p. 569)

The apparent tension between Hilbert's formalism and his wanting to treat it as a defence of the right to claim mathematical existence on the basis of a consistency proof will be considered further in Chapter 5.

If a consistency proof is pointless from Frege's point of view, Hilbert's independence proofs are even more difficult for him to come to terms with. An axiom A is independent of axioms $A_1 \ldots A_n$ if neither it nor its negation is a logical consequence of $A_1 \ldots A_n$. To show that A is a logical consequence of $A_1 \ldots A_n$ all one needs to do is provide a logically correct derivation in which $A_1 \ldots A_n$ are premisses and A is conclusion. But one cannot in the same sort of way demonstrate that A is *not* a logical consequence of $A_1 \ldots A_n$. Hilbert was amongst the first to think in terms of a general method for doing this, a method which is a generalization from the procedure by which the parallel postulate was shown to be independent of the remaining axioms of Euclidean geometry (the same procedure which shows non-Euclidean geometries to be possible). This was done by providing models (such as the surface of a sphere; see pp. 61–2) in which the parallel postulate is false but the remainder of the axioms are true. In the case of the parallel postulate the modelling was initially done within Euclidean geometry; the model for a two-dimensional non-Euclidean geometry is provided by a curved surface describable within three-dimensional Euclidean geometry. But if 'straight line' can be interpreted to mean 'great circle on the surface of a sphere' when constructing models, why should not even less plausible readings be used to generate further models in which other axioms fail?

The answer dpends on how exactly the relation of logical consequence is construed. Frege, in his discussion of Hilbert's independence proofs, was clearly uneasy about the whole procedure. He was not prepared to accept Hilbert's proof as demonstrating independence, even though he did appreciate the importance of the question once it had been raised. The problem is that for Frege relations of logical consequence are relations between thoughts, the determinate senses of sentences. A question about the independence of an axiom A of Euclidean geometry from the remainder is thus, from his point of view, a question about the relation between one self-evident truth about space and others. If A really was not independent then it shouldn't be occupying the place of an axiom, because it is capable of justification from more fundamental truths (hence his appreciation of the significance of the independence question). To reinterpret the terms in the statements in such a way that A becomes false and the remainder of the axioms remain true is to change the thoughts expressed and thus does not give information about the logical relation between the original thoughts.

For Frege, logical laws such as '$F(a)$ v $\neg F(a)$' or '$(F(a)$ & $a = b)$ $\rightarrow F(b)$' are universal laws, holding for all propositions, all objects and all first level concepts. They should therefore not be written as schemata but with appropriate universal quantifiers so that the laws '$\forall\phi$ $\forall x$ $(\phi(x)$ v $\neg\phi(x))$' and '$\forall\phi$ $\forall x$ $\forall y$ $((\phi(x)$ & $x = y)$ $\rightarrow$ $\phi(y))$' themselves express (true) thoughts. The formal character of logic derives, on this view, from its universal applicability, its topic neutrality. This means that in effect it is possible to check that a law has been correctly applied, or an inference has been correctly carried out, without knowing what particular thoughts are expressed by the sentences involved; only their logical structure need be known.

> What is a formal inference? We may say that in a certain sense, every inference is formal in that it proceeds according to a general law of inference; in another sense, every inference is non-formal in that the premises as well as the conclusions have their thought-contents which occur in this particular manner of connection only in that inference.
>
> (Frege 1971 p. 82)

Thus it should, in principle, be possible, even on Frege's view, to provide independence proofs for genuine axioms using reinterpretations of them which preserve their logical forms. Frege's objections to Hilbert's procedures were (i) that his axioms do not express thoughts and are thus not really axioms at all, they are just pseudo propositions, and (ii) that his proofs involve the following reinterpretation:

> let the existence of the equation $ux + vy + w = 0$ mean that the point (x,y) lies on the line $(u:v:w)$.

Here an equation, involving the identity sign, and hence a logical constant, is substituted for the relation of the incidence of a point on a line, which involves no such logical constant. The substitution does not therefore preserve logical form. If, like Frege, one views logic as having laws and a subject matter of its own, where the laws of logic are laws of truth and relations of logical consequence are relations between thoughts, the contents of sentences, then Hilbert's procedures do not amount to proofs. Since logic is not, on this view, purely formal, the ability to discuss the independence of axioms by considering reinterpretations does not extend to the axioms of logic itself. Substitutions involving logical constants (the primitive terms of logic) cannot sensibly be made. So from this standpoint the question of how to prove independence results makes more pressing the need to be clear about what logic is, about what notions, if any, belong to logic. Yet Hilbert could not see the issue in this way for his view of logic is not Frege's. In other words, the logicists, as exemplified by Frege and Russell, had an agenda for supplying a foundation for mathematics which was quite different from Hilbert's.

Frege and Russell shared the view that logical and epistemological foundations coincide. A logical analysis of mathematical propositions is designed to show what the propositions say in such a way that (i) it is possible to trace back to the fundamental principles on which its justification depends, and (ii) its mode of application is clear because it is simply a matter of making an inference according to a law of logic (universal quantifier instantiation). Both would have reason to applaud Hilbert's more complete and more rigorous axiomatization of Euclidean geometry. Frege could accept this as a logical analysis revealing what are the fundamental, self-evident truths grounded in our intuition of space, on which Euclidean geometry rests. Russell could accept it as an important step along the way but since Hilbert leaves as primitive such notions as 'point', 'line' and 'surface' the job is incomplete. These notions must be further analysed (by being defined as constructs of items of possible experience) if it is to be clear what it means to say that physical space is or is not Euclidean. For both Frege and Russell the foundational task is not complete until logical analysis has revealed the content of geometrical propositions by specifying the meanings of basic geometrical terms, for only then can issues of justification for geometrical claims be settled. The purpose of foundational studies is to reveal the first principles from which all remaining mathematics, pure and applied, follows by purely logical deduction.

Hilbert is representative of an alternative approach to the foundations of mathematics, an approach against which both Frege and Russell directed attacks and to which they denied legitimacy, but for different reasons. Hilbert wanted to defend the creative character of mathematics, its ability to develop by creating new theories and new domains of study. Frege denied the possibility of mathematical creativity. The mathematician does not create, he discovers. For Hilbert the vehicle for legitimate, rigorous, but still creative mathematics is the axiomatic method, the postulationism which Russell castigated as having all the advantages of theft over honest toil. Implicit in Russell's criticism is the judgement that mathematics is legitimate only to the extent that it can be applied to the empirical world and that to demonstrate applicability, and hence legitimacy, one must show (a) how it could receive application by defining its primitive terms in such a way that they are either constructs out of items of possible experience or are definable from predicates immediately applicable to such items, and (b) show that under such definitions the primitive propositions either become logical truths or become statements whose conjunction expresses a claim about the empirical world, which can form the antecedent of logical truths saying what would be the case if the antecedent were true.

Hilbert's standards of legitimacy are much less stringent in respect of demonstrating applicability. All that he requires is consistency. An inconsistent theory is of no use and moreover will, if applied, lead to the derivation of false conclusions from true premisses. A consistent theory may have no current uses and one may not be able to see how it might be applied, but it is at least potentially useful and someone may, sooner or later, find applications for it. Application is not here thought to be a matter of logic (applying a universal law to a particular instance), but of finding a model (seeing, for example, that time can be represented by a line and hence treated geometrically). But that should not be part of the mathematician's concern. The key question, from his standpoint, is how to demonstrate consistency, and the key foundational question is whether it is possible to provide any absolute consistency proofs. As we have seen, the logicist programme aims to give such proofs as a part of the reduction of mathematics to logic. The laws of logic correctly stated, must be consistent. In a logically perfect language all terms will have their meaning unambiguously specified and this includes, as Frege emphasized, placing formal restrictions on the procedures for the definition of terms which guarantee that any properly defined term has a reference. Propositions which are proved to be true are therefore true of specified entities (in Russell's case empirical ones) and are thereby guaranteed consistency. The snag is, of course, that Frege's language was not logically perfect and did not ensure consistency. Russell's restrictions on legitimate definition are so restrictive as to make it impossible to legitimate even very basic mathematics without making unjustifiable metaphysical assumptions (Axioms of Infinity and Reducibility).

However, following the pattern of the development of non-Euclidean geometry it is possible to develop relative consistency proofs. Non-Euclidean geometry is proved consistent relative to Euclidean geometry by showing that models of non-Euclidean geometries can be constructed in Euclidean spaces. Euclidean and non-Euclidean geometries can be shown to be consistent relative to the theory of real numbers (that was the aim of the arithmetization of geometry and the elimination of reliance on geometric intuition) at the point when it can be shown that the real numbers can be used to provide models for the axioms of the various geometries. By axiomatizing the assumptions made intuitively about the incidence of points on lines, and treating incidence as a relation between two types of entities, Hilbert made it possible to have objects other than points and lines (e.g. pairs and triples of numbers) standing in this kind of relationship. Hilbert's proof of the consistency of his axiomatization of Euclidean geometry goes via a model constructed within the real numbers and hence is a proof of the consistency of Euclidean geometry relative to the theory of real numbers. The natural follow-up on this approach is to look for a consistency proof for the theory of real numbers and to raise the question of whether there can be any absolute consistency proofs, and what they would look like if they were not a reduction of arithmetic to logic.

FORGING THE FORMAL CHAINS OF REASON

An absolute consistency proof, if there could be such a thing, clearly could not take the form of modelling one theory in another. If arithmetic can suffice for providing models of all other consistent mathematical theories, then it is arithmetic which must be shown to be consistent. The strategy behind Hilbert's 'Programme' was already sketched in 1904. It was to consider arithmetic as a formula game, laying down precisely the rules for constructing well-formed formulae, a list of axioms and rules for constructing proofs of theorems from these axioms, as had already be done, for example, by Peano. Hilbert's idea was that if a notation could be suitably constructed it would be possible to 'see at a glance' whether something was or was not a provable formula, because only formulae with some readily recognizable notational characteristic (such as being equations of the form '$a = b$' with a and b being expressions containing the same number of primitive symbols) would be derivable from the given axioms by the given rules of inference. One would then be able to show that an arithmetically false statement, such as '$0 = 1$', did not have this characteristic and thus was not provable. If the system uses full classical logic it will have the property that from a contradiction anything follows, so finding one unprovable formula suffices to show that no contradiction is provable and hence that the system is consistent. Here formulae are being treated by analogy with algebraic equations, and proof construction becomes a computational process.

Unfortunately for Hilbert, it proved to be much more difficult than he had anticipated to fill in this sketch and provide a philosophical justification of the whole procedure. In a language sufficiently powerful to express arithmetic it is not possible to arrange the notation so that provable formulae are instantly recognizable by virtue of possessing a simple notational characteristic. Hilbert had to be more precise about what needed to be proved consistent, by what means and why. His starting point in arithmetic is very close to Brouwer's; they both cite Kant in urging that arithmetic is grounded in our intuitive grasp of the construction of the series of natural numbers. They differ only in that Brouwer insisted that this is a mental construction, prior to all language and symbolic conventions, whereas Hilbert takes it to be the physical construction involved in writing numbers and numerical formulae. (Both could claim a basis for their position in Kant's work and it would be difficult to adjudicate between them on exegetical grounds since Kant's very sparse remarks about arithmetic are open to more than one reading.) Both are agreed that intuitions derived from the construction of numbers form the foundation for the arithmetic of finite numbers which therefore stands in no need of a consistency proof. The divergence appears when it comes to the question of how to interpret quantification over the whole natural number series, something which is necessary once one moves from arithmetical computation to number theory, to the statement of general principles about numbers. Brouwer insisted that such quantification can be assigned a meaning based on our grasp of the nature of the number series as potentially infinite and that this is the only way in which meaning can be assigned. This means that the law of the excluded middle cannot be regarded as holding in general for propositions of the form '$\forall n\ F(n)$', where n ranges over the natural numbers. Goldbach's conjecture that every even number can be expressed as the sum of two primes, for example, cannot be asserted to be either true or false in advance of our being able to produce constructions which will decide it and it is possible that it might remain forever undecided.

Hilbert, on the other hand, was not prepared to trade the simplicity of classical logic for the complications introduced by Brouwer and was not prepared to forgo the principle of excluded middle.

> Taking the principle of the excluded middle from the mathematician would be the same, say, as proscribing the telescope to the astronomer or to the boxer the use of his fists. To prohibit existence statements and the principle of excluded middle is tantamount to relinquishing the science of mathematics altogether.
>
> (Hilbert 1927 p. 476)

Hilbert preserves the law of excluded middle by regarding quantified formulae as mere formulae, as introducing ideal elements (analogous to the point at infinity of projective geometry, or to i as the square root of -1) whose meaning is given only by the role they play in the system, not by any intuitions. This way of describing it is more natural for Hilbert than for Frege and Russell because he does not introduce the universal and existential quantifiers directly. Instead the 'ideal element' is introduced by his ε-symbol. Assuming the law of excluded middle, then for any given property $A(x)$ of numbers (e.g. x is prime) either

i there is a number n for which $A(n)$ is true, or
ii there is no such number.

In either case there must be a representative number, r, such that for every number n, $A(n) \to A(r)$, for if (i) is the case, take r to be one of the numbers for which $A(x)$ holds, and if (ii) is the case, assign r a random value (r is a number which is A if anything is, for example, 2 is even if anything is, 3 is the largest prime number if anything is). The selection of such a representative r is expressed by Hilbert's ε-operator. In this way the choice function, a function which picks an element from any given set, is thus built into the ε-operator. The axiom implicitly defining this ideal element is

$$A(n) \to A(\varepsilon_x A(x)).$$

The two usual quantifiers can then be defined.

$$\exists x \, A(x) \equiv_{df} A(\varepsilon_x A(x)) \qquad \forall x \, A(x) \equiv_{df} A(\varepsilon_x \neg A(x)).$$

Hilbert went on to distinguish between *real propositions*, finitary propositions asserting relations between specific numbers (e.g. '2 + 3 > 2 + 1', '2 × 3 = 6'), *finitarily significant propositions*, such as 'for any given number n, $n + 1 = 1 + n$', and *ideal propositions* which are expressed using the ε-symbol and which do not have a finitary meaning, e.g. '$\varepsilon_n(n + 1 \neq 1 + n) + 1 = 1 + \varepsilon_n(n + 1 \neq 1 + n)$'. The negation of a finitarily significant general proposition , for example 'there is a number n for which $2n$ is not expressible as the sum of two primes', is not finitarily significant because there is no bound placed on n, and this means that finitary checking through cases need never terminate; failure to have found a counter-example does not mean that no counter-example exists. So, whereas '$\exists n \leqslant m \, A(n)$' is finitarily significant, '$\exists n \, A(n)$' (or '$A(\varepsilon_x A(x))$') is not. Thus sentences containing ε-terms are to be regarded as mere formulae, lacking finitary significance; they are part of the calculation/reasoning machinery, introduced to make it run more smoothly, but they have no finitary meaning to call their own.

Hilbert saw the step from '$1 + n = n + 1$' to '$1 + \varepsilon_n(1 + n \neq 1 + n) = \varepsilon_n(1 + n \neq n + 1) + 1$' by analogy with that from '$2 + 3 = 3 + 2$', a perfectly definite numerical proposition, to '$a + b = b + a$', an algebraic schema which on its own expresses no specific proposition. His problem was how to justify this procedure (and the assumption of the law of excluded middle on which it rests). In the case of arithmetic it will be justified, or at least be seen to do no harm, if (a) the formal system is formally consistent, no contradiction can be proved in it, and (b) the proofs of finitarily

106

significant formulae which go via ideal propositions do not lead to the derivation of any false propositions.

> There is just one condition, albeit an absolutely necessary one, connected with the method of ideal elements. That condition is a *proof of consistency*, for the extension of a domain by the addition of ideal elements is legitimate only if the extension does not cause contradictions to appear in the old, narrower domain, or, in other words, only if the relations that obtain among the old structures when the ideal structures are deleted are always valid in the old domain.
>
> (Hilbert 1925 p. 199)

Now it is part and parcel of the notion of a real proposition that it can in principle be checked by computation and that computation can be regarded in either a contentual or a merely formal light. Thus any such proposition which is provable via ideal propositions must, if the ideal system is consistent, also be in principle checkable by finite calculation. In this respect, if the system **I**, with ideal elements, is consistent it must be a conservative extension of the finitary system. One of the more remarkable products of work inspired by Hilbert's Programme was the consolidation and clarification in the characterization of what counts as effective computability. The task of characterizing the arithmetic functions which are effectively computable has been approached from a variety of directions all of which have been proved to isolate the same class of functions. This gives added weight to the sense that here at least we are not dealing with artefacts of any particular theory or any particular notation. This situation led Church to propose his thesis that all effectively computable functions are recursive (see the end of the chapter for a definition). If Church's thesis is accepted then the requirement for a formal system **I** of infinitary arithmetic to be a conservative extension of finitary arithmetic can be given a more precise form. If A is a real proposition and **I** $\vdash$ A then PRA $\vdash$ A, where PRA is Primitive Recursive Arithmetic.

The position is not so clear, however, *vis-à-vis* finitarily significant general propositions, those expressed in **I** by formulae using universal quantifiers and containing no unbounded existential quantifiers or negated universal quantifiers. Such formulae can have finitary significance but cannot necessarily be shown by finite computations to be either true or false. Not all such propositions

are effectively decidable, only their instances are. So the requirement that the system with ideal elements not lead to the deduction
of false, finitarily significant propositions does not determine
whether this is supposed to require a conservative extension of
PRA (only allow proof of effectively decidable general propositions), or whether it would allow for genuine, non-conservative
extension of PRA (allow proofs of general propositions not
provable by other means, but whose instances must indeed be
correct when checked by calculation). In the statement of
'Hilbert's Programme' as made precise by others such as Weyl and
von Neumann, it is assumed that the requirement here is for
conservative extension. But it is not clear that this was Hilbert's
original intention. There is a sense in which a consistency proof is
only really interesting if it legitimates the use of machinery which
will get us something that we could not get by other means. Von
Neumann restates Hilbert's Programme as follows:

1. To enumerate all the symbols used in mathematics and logic.
These symbols, called 'primitive symbols', include the symbols '—' and '⇒' (which stand for negation and implication).
2. To characterize unambiguously all the combinations of
these symbols which represent statements classified as
'meaningful' in classical mathematics. These combinations
are called 'formulas' . . .
3. To supply a construction procedure which enables us to
construct successively all the formulas which correspond to
the 'provable' statements of classical mathematics. This
procedure, accordingly, is called 'proving'.
4. To show (in a finitary combinatorial way) that those
formulas which correspond to statements of classical mathematics which can be checked by finitary arithmetical methods
can be proved (i.e. constructed) by the process described in
(3) if and only if the check of the corresponding statement
shows it to be true.

To accomplish tasks 1–4 would be to establish the validity
of classical mathematics as a short-cut method for validating
arithmetical statements whose elementary validation would
be much too tedious. But since this is in fact the way we use
mathematics, we would at the same time sufficiently establish
the empirical validity of classical mathematics.

(von Neumann 1931 p. 63)

This restatement is justified as an interpretation of a remark made by Hilbert (1925 p. 184).

> Just as operations with the infinitely small were replaced by operations with the finite which yielded exactly the same results and led to exactly the same elegant formal relationships, so in general must deductive methods based on the infinite be replaced by finite procedures which yield exactly the same results; i.e. which make possible the same chains of proofs and the same methods of getting formulas and theorems.

But it is worth noting how far this statement of what would be achieved by producing a finitary consistency proof for classical arithmetic has drifted from the conception implicit in Hilbert's dispute with Frege. Hilbert's project has been assimilated to the empiricist programme for the justification of the use of mathematics in physical theories without thereby having to countenance the existence of abstract entities, mathematical knowledge or any non-empirical intuition. Mathematical reasoning is viewed simply as the mechanical manipulation of meaningless symbols. In this way the formalist programme comes to be seen as a way of finally dispelling the idea that there is any creative potential in mathematical reasoning. But Hilbert had seen consistency proofs as a way of grounding existence claims for abstract objects and thus of vindicating the creative power of mathematical reasoning.

In 1–3 von Neumann is expressing the requirement that classical mathematics be written in the language of a formal system in the modern, technical sense, i.e. a system which consists of an alphabet of symbols, recursive syntactical rules for the legitimate combination of symbols into finite strings (well-formed formulae) and recursive rules for constructing sequences of well-formed formulae (to be called proofs). The rules in both cases are required to be such that it must be effectively decidable whether a given sequence of symbols or of formulae has or has not been constructed in accordance with the rules. This is precisely the sort of language which can be fed into a computer, and a computer will be able to generate formulae and 'proofs' according to the rules and to check strings presented to it for correctness. As von Neumann remarks, much of the work required to write mathematics into this kind of language had already been done by Russell and Whitehead, even though they did not view their logical language as a strictly formal, uninterpreted symbol system of this kind.

SUCCESSES AND FAILURES

Part of the difficulty in arriving at any clear statement of what was actually required for the provision of an absolute consistency proof for arithmetic by the proof-theoretic route which Hilbert had suggested was that it entailed sorting out the relations between syntactic and semantic notions in a way which had not, up to that point, been attempted because there was nothing to make questions about these relationships particularly pressing. Hilbert himself slid from syntactic to semantic notions of consistency, logical consequence and completeness without apparently noticing the transition, as when he took proof of formal consistency to be ground for asserting the existence of entities of which the axioms of the formally consistent theory are true. Much of the early work on formal systems, work which prepared the ground for Gödel's theorem, consisted in clarifying and/or reforging key logical notions in semantic and syntactic versions and then investigating their relations. This is well documented in van Heijenhoort (1967). Here a brief summary of the results most relevant to Hilbert's Programme will be given prior to a more detailed discussion of their implications. For more complete expositions of these results and of Gödel's theorem in particular, the reader is referred to the further reading suggested for this chapter, as many excellent expositions are available.

1 1915 – Löwenheim proved that if a finitely valid well-formed formula of first order predicate calculus is not valid, i.e. if there is some infinite domain in which it is not satisfiable, then there is a denumerable domain in which it is not satisfiable.

2 1920 and 1922 – Skolem improved on Löwenheim's result showing (1920) that if F is a formula containing no individual constant and no free variables then, if there is a domain D in which F is satisfiable, F is satisfiable in a denumerable subdomain of D, the same meaning being assigned to the predicate letters in F in both cases. In 1922 he proved that, if F is satisfiable, it is satisfiable in the domain of natural numbers.

3 1930 – Gödel proved the completeness of first order predicate calculus; i.e. that every valid well-formed formula (one which

is satisfied in all possible interpretations) is provable. In other words, every well-formed formula is either refutable or satisfiable in some interpretation. He also proved the Compactness Theorem, that every set S of sentences which is such that every finite subset of S is satisfiable is itself satisfiable.

4 1931 – Gödel proved (i) that any formal system, such as that of *Principia Mathematica* (PM), in which arithmetic can be expressed, must contain a sentence G such that if PM is consistent then neither G nor $\neg$G is a theorem of PM so that G is undecidable in PM, and (ii) that if PM is consistent the formal consistency of PM cannot be proved by means formalizable within PM.

5 1931 – Tarski showed that it is not possible to define within a finitary meta-theory for a system such as PM a predicate which is satisfied by all and only the true sentences of PM.

6 1936 – Church proved that there can be no algorithm to determine whether a given formula written in the language of first order predicate calculus is or is not provable in that calculus.

7 1936 – Gentzen proved the consistency of a formal system of arithmetic using transfinite induction up to ε_0, the first infinite ordinal number α such that $\omega^\alpha = \alpha$.

8 1974 – Chaitin proved that in any given formal system, in order to show that a string of symbols is of complexity m, it is necessary to use axioms which already have complexity greater than $m + c$, where c is a constant independent of the axioms, see DelaHaye (1989).

9 1976 – Friedman uses 'reverse mathematics' to obtain partial realizations of Hilbert's Programme, see Simpson (1988).

10 1977 – Paris and Harrington produce a mathematical incompleteness in first order arithmetic (PA) by defining a rapidly growing computable function whose computability is not provable in PA.

11 1987 – Chaitin wrote a diophantine equation containing 17,000 variables which is not solvable in any formal system.

Results 1–3 appeared to vindicate Hilbert's strategy. 1 and 2 show that arithmetic can be used to provide models for all first order theories which have models and thus that an absolute consistency proof for arithmetic might provide a means for showing any mathematical theory to be consistent by constructing an arithmetical model for it. However, (i) the connection between being formally consistent and having a model had yet to be made, and (ii) Skolem's 1920 result has apparently paradoxical results for set theory in that it entails that if set theory has any standard models (ones in which sets are sets and 'ϵ' really is the membership relation) then it has a standard model whose universe is denumerable. But it is possible to prove within axiomatic set theory the existence of non-denumerable sets. The appearance of paradox here can be partially dissolved by noting that the non-denumerability of a set S is defined as the non-existence of a one–one correspondence between S and any subset of the natural numbers. Rather 'small' models of the set theoretic universe can therefore make sets 'look' non-denumerable because the model simply does not contain the one–one correspondences that can be seen to exist from outside the model and which would prove denumerability (see Tiles 1989: Chapter 8). It remains the case, however, that the first order axiomatization of set theory considered formally, even with standard notions of set and set membership, cannot provide a definition of any of the transfinite cardinalities beyond $\aleph_0$ in that it cannot fix them in any absolute way. The question of what can or should be the significance attached to statements about such numbers is thus rendered very much an open question.

The completeness theorem for first order predicate calculus, (3), justifies, for first order theories, moves between semantic and syntactic senses of consistency and consequence by demonstrating their extensional equivalence. But the proof of this result is not strictly finitistic, and this is not surprising since the articulation of the semantic concepts on which it depends is not finitary. A valid wff of first order predicate calculus is one which is satisfiable in all domains and under all interpretations of its predicates, and the domain of all possible interpretations for predicates is not merely infinite, but non-denumerably infinite. Indeed, Gödel's comment on the significance of his completeness theorem is that it has the effect of reducing the problem of deciding whether a formula is valid from one concerned with the non-denumerable totality of possible interpretations to that of the denumerable totality of formal proofs. There are by now various strategies for proving this completeness result, but in one way or another they depend on using the properties of formal derivability in a language extended by the addition of a denumerable list of new individual constants to construct for any wff A which is not provable an interpretation in which ¬A is satisfied. This is done by constructing a set S, which will be infinite, of quantifier-free sentences which are derivable from A (and hence required to be satisfied if A is) and which are together just sufficient to ensure that if they are all true then A is satisfied. The proof that the construction of S does in fact yield a set of sentences which can be simultaneously satisfied is non-finitary. This raises a question as to whether the restriction to finitary methods was either the correct or the only possible way to formulate the formalist programme. If the restriction to finitary methods is imposed, then questions must be raised about what can be the status, from a formalist point of view, of semantic notions and of proofs such as the completeness proof. Perhaps the formalist should, as some did, eschew such notions altogether and stick strictly to the finitary, to the computable and the formal. This would indeed be to turn mathematics into a formula game and would involve (a) abandoning the vision of mathematics which Hilbert had hoped to justify, and (b) making the whole question of how formalizations ever get application and with what justification almost unaskable. At this stage the point of looking for a consistency proof disappears into a project of turning mathematics into computation and the finitary theory of computation which is concerned not so much with logic as with algorithms, programmes and information.

On the other hand, the spirit of this non-finitary proof is highly formalistic and conforms to a strategy outlined by Hilbert in a discussion of what would be required to show the consistency of an axiom system.

> IV If we want to investigate a given system of axioms according to the principles above, we must distribute the combinations of the objects taken as primitive into two classes, that of entities and that of non-entities, with the axioms playing the role of prescriptions that the partition must satisfy. The main difficulty will consist in recognizing the possibility of distributing all objects into the two classes, that of entities and that of non-entities. The question whether this distribution is possible is essentially equivalent to the question whether the consequences we can obtain from the axioms by specialization and combination lead to a contradiction or not.
>
> (Hilbert 1904 p. 135)

(Here 'objects' are symbols and their legitimate combinations and 'entities' are those which are to be interpreted as 'true'.) Tarski's theorem (5) is a result of following up on this idea. Tarski first made precise what are the syntactic (morphological) conditions that have to be satisfied before a given set of sentences in a formalized language can be designated the set of 'true' sentences of that language and how this could be linked to their intended interpretation. Formal, recursive semantics has its origins in Tarski's work. For example, the set Tr of 'true' sentences of any language must be deductively closed (in other words if $S_1 \in$ Tr and $S_1 \vdash S_2$, then $S_2 \in$ Tr), but in addition Tarski required (in his Material Adequacy Condition) that one must be able to prove, for each sentence S of the language in question, that $S \in$ Tr iff p, where p is the proposition expressed by the sentence designated by the name 'S'. Tarski was then able to prove that a consistent formal language for arithmetic cannot consistently be extended to include a definition of truth for its own sentences. Intuitively this is because a version of the Liar Paradox would be formalizable in the extended language. Suppose a formal language L for arithmetic is extended to a language L^+ which includes the formal syntax of L^+. The wffs of L^+ can be listed and assigned numbers on the basis of this ordering; any 'truth' predicate will thus correspond to a predicate '$P(n)$' of numbers, i.e. $S \in$ Tr iff $P(s)$, where s is the number assigned to S. Let $sub(x,y)$ be the number of the sentence which results from substituting the numeral 'y' for the free variable in the formula whose number is x if this formula contains just one free variable and 0 otherwise. Let the number assigned to '$\neg P(sub(x,x))$' be t, and let T be the sentence '$\neg P(sub(t,t))$'; then $P(sub(t,t))$ iff $T \in$ Tr , i.e iff '$\neg P(sub(t,t))$' $\in$ Tr, but then, by the Material Adequacy Condition, we should have $\neg P(sub(t,t))$. Hence $\neg T$ iff T, and either the formal language for arithmetic is inconsistent or the definition of 'truth' is not materially adequate.

Tarski's contribution was to clarify semantic notions in a formalistic but non-finitary way. Gödel's results, (4), had a more immediate impact on Hilbert's Programme because the methods used are finitary and combinatorial. The limitations that would be imposed on one trying to conduct strictly finitary meta-theory became clearer with the publication of Gödel's 'On Formally Undecidable Propositions of Principia Mathematica and Related Systems', which is perhaps one of the most discussed and disputed papers in the philosophy of mathematics. Some say that it brings a definitive halt to Hilbert's quest for an absolute consistency proof; others argue that it does not. Some have interpreted it as demonstrating that the human mind is not a machine; others say it has no such implications. Clearly assessment of the impact of Gödel's results on Hilbert's position depends crucially not only on the interpretation of Gödel's proofs but also on how one formulates Hilbert's Programme.

What Gödel first proved was that any formal system, such as that of PM, in which arithmetic can be expressed must contain a sentence G such that if PM is consistent neither G nor ¬G are theorems of PM. In other words, a consistent formalization of arithmetic cannot also be complete; it must always leave some sentences undecided. If one believes that every arithmetic sentence is either true or false, then one will see this theorem as having the further consequence of entailing that any consistent formalization of arithmetic will be an inadequate basis for proving all true arithmetic propositions. Moreover, Gödel's proof itself shows how, for any given formal system, one can descriptively identify one such unprovable proposition (which will be in the form of a diophantine equation). Gödel went on to derive, as a corollary, the conclusion that if a formal system such as PM is consistent its formal consistency cannot be proved by means formalizable within the system.

The strategy behind the proof of Gödel's first incompleteness theorem built on and indeed constituted a vindication of Hilbert's own view that formal logic cannot serve as a foundation for arithmetic because the development of a formal symbolic language rests on the same intuitions that ground arithmetic. Gödel used a coding device, now known as gödel-numbering, which codes every primitive symbol of the formal language by a prime number (e.g. '0' – 1, '¬' – 3, '→' – 5, '∀' – 7, '(' – 11, ')' – 13, . . .), so that every string of primitive symbols corresponds to a string of prime numbers, say, $n_1, \ldots, n_k$. Each such string is then coded into a single number $2^{n_1} . 3^{n_2} . \ldots, p_k^{n_k}$, where p_n is the nth prime number. (The original string can be retrieved by factorization and knowledge of the code.) Each sequence of formulae is then coded into a string of numbers and the process can be repeated to get a single number coding a whole sequence of formulae. Gödel then shows that the properties of being a well-formed formula, of being a wff which results from substituting the numeral 'n' in the wff containing a single free variable and with gödel-number m and of being a provable wff translate into effectively definable arithmetical properties of numbers. The property of being a provable wff of PM is thus expressible in PM itself by an arithmetical predicate. In fact there will be a predicate $\exists x \, \text{Bew}(x, \text{sub}(y,z))$ saying 'there is a number x which is the number of a proof of the formula obtained by substituting the numeral y for the free variable in the formula whose number is z'. Consider $\neg\exists x \, \text{Bew}(x, \text{sub}(y,y))$. It will have a gödel-number, say g. Then let G be $\neg\exists x \, \text{Bew}(x, \text{sub}(g,g))$ which 'says' that there is no proof of the formula which results from substituting the numeral g in the formula whose gödel-number is g, i.e. that G itself is not provable. Then neither G nor $\neg$G can be theorems of PM. If G were provable, i.e. if PM $\vdash$ G, there would have to be a proof and one would also have PM $\vdash \exists x \, \text{Bew}(x, \text{sub}(g,g))$, i.e. PM $\vdash \neg$G. If $\neg$G were provable, we would have PM $\vdash \exists x \, \text{Bew}(x, \text{sub}(g,g))$, and if all arithmetic theorems of PM are true of the natural numbers (if PM is ω-consistent) there must be a number which is the number of a proof of G. In either case PM would not be formally consistent.

Gödel's whole proof uses only finitary reasoning. In principle, therefore, it could, with sufficient coding, be conducted in PM itself as a proof of an arithmetical proposition which could also be interpreted as saying that, if there is no wff such that both it and its negation are both theorems of PM, then neither G nor $\neg$G are theorems of PM. If the arithmetic statement corresponding to the statement that PM is formally consistent could be proved in PM, then PM $\vdash \neg\exists x \, \text{Bew}(x, \text{sub}(g,g))$, i.e. PM $\vdash$ G, contrary to the result of the first theorem. In other words the formal consistency of a formal system for classical arithmetic cannot be proved by means formalizable within that system, if the system is indeed formally consistent.

How much of Hilbert's Programme survives these results? How much of the programme outlined by von Neumann survives? The first incompleteness theorem has more immediate impact on the logicist programmes of Frege and Russell than on Hilbert's Programme. It does mean that if one hangs on to bivalence and the law of excluded middle for arithmetic propositions, then the reduction of arithmetic to logic will always be incomplete. Hilbert, on the other hand, although he was committed to the view that every well-posed mathematical problem has a solution, was not committed to the view that every arithmetical problem would be soluble by the methods available within a single formal system.

In fact one of the principal attractions of tackling a mathematical problem is that we always hear this cry within us: There is the problem, find the answer; you can find it just by thinking, for there is no *ignorabimus* in mathematics. Now my theory of proof cannot supply a general method for solving every mathematical problem – there is no such method. Still the proof (that the assumption that every mathematical problem is solvable is a consistent assumption) falls completely within the scope of our theory.

(Hilbert 1925 p. 200)

Solving a problem meant, for him, getting a yes or no answer or showing that no answer could be given within the framework within which the problem was posed. 'Solutions' of the latter kind characteristically require methods drawn from outside the framework. There are suggestions that Hilbert did think that axiomatizations of geometry and arithmetic should be complete in the sense that all models be isomorphic (and the axioms categorical) and he was not averse to using higher order axioms to ensure this. Second order arithmetic is complete in this sense, i.e. if A is the conjunction of the (finite) list of second order axioms for arithmetic and T is an arithmetic sentence (possibly G), then either all interpretations in which n-place predicates range over all sets of ordered n-tuples of objects in the domain of the interpretation which render A true (which are a model for A) make T true, or they all make $\neg$T true. Gödel's theorem then entails that there are valid second order wffs, one of ('A $\rightarrow$ G', or 'A $\rightarrow$ $\neg$G') for example, which are not formally provable. So the demand for categorical axiomatizations is not incompatible with allowing for the non-closure of formal techniques for answering questions about the structure so axiomatized.

If, on the other hand, we follow up the clarification of Hilbert's Programme along the lines indicated by von Neumann (see, for example, Simpson 1988) it becomes the project of getting a finitistically correct consistency proof (one carried out in PRA) for second order arithmetic (Z_2). If this could be done, any finitarily significant general wff, one containing only finitely bounded existential quantification and unrestricted universal quantification over the natural numbers, that was provable in Z_2 would also be provable (in principle) in PRA. Gödel's first incompleteness theorem (together with the categoricity of Z_2) definitively shows

117

that Z_2 is not a conservative extension of PRA. So if that was Hilbert's Programme, if the Programme was that of *reducing* infinitistic mathematics to finitistic mathematics, it definitively failed.

In many respects it does not matter what exactly Hilbert's Programme was; it probably never was an exact programme but was an initially vague, possibly confused but exceedingly fruitful idea which was capable of being clarified in various ways. The point of re-examining his work and the results it spawned is not that of pure historical exegesis, it is to see where exactly we now stand, what are and are not viable options in the philosophy of mathematics. Gödel's first incompleteness theorem suffices to show that reductivist positions, whether logicist or finitist–formalist, are not viable. But it does not, by itself, rule out non-reductivist or less strictly finitist versions of Hilbertian formalism.

The import of Gödel's second incompleteness theorem on these options is harder to assess. At one level the theorem seems straightforward. If finitary methods are those of PRA, these can all be represented within PM, in which case Gödel has proved that the consistency of PM cannot be proved by finitary methods. One complication is that work by Fefferman has shown that care is needed in defining the arithmetical counterpart of the consistency predicate because Gödel's result does not hold for all ways of doing this. If there is a definition of consistency under which the consistency of a formal system is provable within that system, as Fefferman shows for some systems, does that mean that Hilbert's Programme can after all be carried out? The answer would appear to be 'No' (see Resnik 1988) because in order to recognize that this new formalization of consistency does indeed express consistency one would already need to know that the system was consistent in Gödel's sense. So what Fefferman shows is that if his systems are consistent in Gödel's sense then there is also another sense of consistency in which consistency can be proved within the system. This does not yet provide an absolute consistency proof. But it does mean that in order to defend the definitive character of Gödel's result one would need to argue to the effect that Gödel's characterization of consistency is correct and natural in some sense in which Fefferman's is not.

This whole discussion points up another query about the tenability of the finitist–formalist's position for again he has a problem of how to attach finitistic significance either to the statement that a given sentence in a formal system of arithmetic is provable or to the statement that it is not. The former, as expressed by the 'Bew' predicate, is an unrestricted existential statement and the latter a universal statement. If the formalist is going to refuse to avail himself of the intuitionist account of quantifiers when working in his finitary meta-theory, he is going to have trouble making any sense of the proof-theoretic notions he needs to employ. The issue is sensitive in this case because for any given number n there will be a finitary proof that $\neg Bew(n, sub(g,g))$. But this is what Hilbert thought was the finitary significance of a general proposition about numbers, and if that is so, why does it not count as sufficient grounds for asserting the general proposition? Hilbert gives us no basis for answering this question, whereas the intuitionist can say what is lacking – what we lack is an effective procedure which will, for any n, generate a proof (or the number of a proof) of $\neg Bew(n, sub(g,g))$.

But if the formalist has to allow his finitary meta-theory to expand in the direction indicated by intuitionist mathematics, admitting the significance of the potentially infinite, then again it is not clear that inability to prove the consistency of PM by methods formalizable within PM entails not being able to prove consistency by finitary means. It is along these lines that Gentzen produced his consistency proof. He argued that there are forms of reasoning which are not strictly finitary, but which are essentially constructive and therefore more reliable than those which are available in full classical arithmetic.

The results of both Gödel and Church demonstrate that Hilbert was mistaken in thinking that it might be possible, by suitable selection of notation, to have a formal system which was both sufficiently complex to be capable of being interpreted as a formalization of classical arithmetic and yet in which theorems would be recognizable as such on the basis of possession of some relatively simple morphological characteristic. Church's theorem shows that even though first order predicate calculus is complete, i.e. every valid wff is provable, there is no finitary procedure which will test for provability (and hence validity). Gentzen's detailed work in proof theory shows why this is the case. The basic problem is that the syntactic complexity of a wff is no guide to the possible syntactic complexity of a proof of it. If it were possible to put an upper bound on the length and/or complexity of a proof required to prove a given wff based on its own syntactic complexity, then there would be only a large but finite number of proofs to check through before concluding that the wff either was or was not provable. But proofs of relatively simple formulae can go via formulae which are much more complex. Gentzen's basic idea was to present proofs in a form in which as far as possible the inference rules only allow for the derivation of syntactically more complex wffs from syntactically less complex ones. Much of the work of his consistency proof consists in showing how ordinary proofs can be transformed into proofs which are of this kind. The idea behind his proof is close to Hilbert's original basis for thinking that a consistency proof could be obtained by looking at proofs. This was that to show the consistency of a formal theory for arithmetic one merely needed to show that '0 = 1' cannot be proved. One naturally thinks that if there is any proof of such a simple sentence, there must be one which is really short and simple and should thus be easy to check for. Gentzen's idea was to show that this idea is, at bottom, correct by showing how any proof can be reduced to a 'direct' proof (a proof which he saw as revealing the finitary content of the proposition proved). In the case of '0 = 1' its direct proof would be very short – the only direct proof for a numerical equation is a computation. So if finite computations do not yield '0 = 1', the full system of arithmetic will not. The work lies in developing the sense of 'direct proof' and proving that reduction can always be carried out. In the process Gentzen had to allow his 'direct' proofs to be denumerable infinite. Difficulties arise because '0 = 1' might be proved via (possibly repeated) instantiations of some general propositions $\forall x \, F(x)$, which was in turn arrived at by complete induction, $(F(0) \, \& \, \forall x \, (F(x) \rightarrow F(x + 1))) \rightarrow \forall x \, F(x)$, or by use of the Cut Rule, which is a generalization of $A \rightarrow B$, $B \rightarrow C \vdash A \rightarrow C$. What has to be shown is that if '0 = 1' could be proved by this kind of route, it could also be proved 'more directly' without using these rules. Gentzen uses Cantor's transfinite ordinal numbers $0 \ldots n \ldots \omega, \omega + 1 \ldots \omega + \omega, \ldots \omega.\omega \ldots \omega^\omega \ldots$ up to ε_0, which is the limit of this sequence, to provide a measure of the complexity of his proof structures. The point about proof structures is that they cannot be linearly ordered, like the natural numbers, but form trees. Each of the numbers up to ε_0 corresponds to a well-ordering of the natural numbers and so there is a respect in which the theory of these numbers could be argued to be still part of constructive, if not finitary, arithmetic. Their use does not involve any non-denumerable totalities so that Gentzen's consistency proof does constitute a reduction from the non-denumerable to the denumerable.

The results of Gentzen and Church both point in the direction of suggesting that Hilbert's hope that powerful notation would make recognition of consistency easy, whilst at the same time allowing for the expression of complex mathematical concepts, is flawed. There is a closer connection between the characteristics of a notation and the structures that can be characterized by means of concepts expressed in it than perhaps Hilbert recognized. This is both a plus and a minus from the point of view of some kind of formalism as a philosophy of mathematics. It may dash hopes of an absolute consistency proof, but on the other hand a study of the connection between notational complexity and expressive power should clearly be at the heart of any non-reductionist formalism.

Chaitin's work uses results and techniques from the field of algorithmic information theory and work which produced a negative solution of Hilbert's tenth problem. There is no algorithm that enables one to state whether a diophantine equation has solutions, contrary to Hilbert's expectations. As previously remarked, the domain of the computable has come to have a privileged status not just because of its association with formalism, or the mechanized image of reason, but because, like arithmetic itself, it has shown that it is not system (or language) relative. In algorithmic information theory the 'information content' or 'complexity' of a statement composed of a string of symbols is defined to be equal to the size of the smallest computer programme that permits one to generate it. In a sufficiently powerful programming language one can show that a string is simple by producing a small programme capable of writing it. The first one thousand digits of $010101\ldots$ is simple; the first one hundred thousand digits in the decimal expansion of π is still relatively simple because it can be generated by a programme which is shorter than it. By applying these ideas to formal systems Chaitin proved his 1974 result which shows that in a certain sense an axiomatic system cannot produce theorems richer in complexity than the axioms themselves. Chaitin produces his unsolvable diophantine equation by encoding into it a problem already known to be undecidable with the result that the equation is so complex that the only way to resolve m cases is to put an amount of information equal to m in the system of axioms at the outset.

Here we have an illustration of the way in which expressive (or representational) power outstrips the computational or decision making power. The same applies to the Paris–Harrington results. Define a set S of integers to be 'large' iff the number of elements in S is not less that the smallest $n \in S$ (e.g. {3, 10, 19} is 'large', whereas {20, 22, 24, 27, 31} is not, since it contains less than 20 elements). Paris and Harrington proved that, if given a big enough set S of integers and an assignment of colours, such as red or blue, to each pair of members of S, there is a 'large' set all of whose pairs are blue. And more generally, for any given c and k, if S is big enough and c colours are assigned to k-tuples of members of S, there is a 'large' set all of whose k-tuples are of the same colour. They also showed, by giving models, that this theorem is independent of first order arithmetic.

The significance of this result derives from the fact that it is a genuinely arithmetical statement which is shown to be undecidable; moreover it is one which has the form $\forall x \, \exists y \, A(x,y)$, where $A(x,y)$ is a provably decidable predicate. In such a case if $\forall x \, \exists y \, A(x,y)$ were provable there would be a provably computable function $f(x)$ such that $\forall x \, A(x,f(x))$. The trouble in the Paris–Harrington case is that the function $f(x)$ which would be required here is computable (hence the theorem is known to be true) but not provably computable because it is a function which grows too rapidly.

Friedman has produced a function which grows even more rapidly than the one required by the Paris–Harrington theorem. In addition he has developed an approach which he calls 'reverse mathematics' which is the project of finding out exactly what axioms are required to prove a given arithmetic theorem by working backwards from the theorem, deducing axioms from it. This is not a wholly novel mathematical strategy; it is Pappus' method of analysis, the method which Descartes sought to revive (see p. 14), revamped and made more sophisticated by the addition of complicated coding procedures. Freidman is using this approach not to prove the theorems themselves, but to determine which subsystems of second order arithmetic are conservative extensions of PRA with respect to sentences containing only unnegated universal quantification. In this sense he is getting partial realizations of Hilbert's Programme as made precise by von Neumann. The point of this research is not principally to vindicate Hilbert, but to clarify the role of strong set existence axioms in ordinary mathematics. How much, if any, of the arithmetic of the natural numbers is affected by assumptions made concerning the existence or non-existence of these large sets? The results from the reverse mathematics programme show that there is a large part of classical mathematics which is not affected by these assumptions, a large part which can be carried out in a subsystem of second order arithmetic which is a conservative extension of PRA. But if Hilbert wanted conservative extension it also had to be established by finitary means. Without getting into details of the proof procedures used by Friedman one cannot say what should be the finitist–formalist attitude toward his results. Since many of his theorems are not finitarily stated and the model theory used is not finitary, the status of such results as realization of Hilbert's Programme is questionable. If the restriction to strict finitary formalism is removed then the requirement to demonstrate conservative extension also goes, so the philosophical significance of such results is not clear. On the other hand this kind of investigation would seem to be a good example of the sort of mathematical work advocated by Hilbert for clarifying the axiomatic foundations of the subject. Hilbert did regard it as important to determine as precisely as possible which axioms were required for proving a particular result, and was the first to introduce model-theoretic techniques for pursuing this type of investigation. The mathematical investigation of formal systems has come a long way, and continues; the philosophical investigation seems to have ground to a halt. To get a clearer impression of how things now stand it is perhaps best to recap on Hilbert's philosophical position.

LOGIC AND ITS LIMITATIONS

Hilbert's early approach to providing a foundation for the axiomatic method was model theoretic (or semantic). That is, he proved the consistency of a set of axioms by providing a model. He then assumed that no contradiction could be derived from the axioms provided that no contradiction could be derived within the theory which supplies the model. Thus geometry is proved consistent relative to the theory of real numbers. Hilbert was interested in consistency because he took it that provided an axiom system is consistent, the structure (or class of structures) they define exists and the axioms can be seen as expressing truths about this structure (or class of structures). Implicit in the significance attached to this method of proof as used in the context of geometry is the thought that the model proving consistency is not identical to the structure in question. The real numbers with an appropriately defined set of relations are not Euclidean space. To show that they can provide a model for geometric axioms is not to reduce geometry to the theory of real numbers. The point about implicit definitions provided by axiom systems is that they are non-reductive. The problem, raised by Frege, is that Hilbert needed to justify his claim that a consistency proof for his axiomatization of Euclidean geometry gives him the right to claim the existence of Euclidean space as a mathematical structure distinct from models of the axioms. Hilbert, on the other hand, saw the primary problem as being that of providing an absolute consistency proof of the theory of real numbers.

The tack taken for trying to prove absolute consistency reverses the priority of syntax and semantics; the task is to show that arithmetic with infinitary quantification is formally consistent, in the sense that no contradiction can be proved. A proof of the formal consistency of arithmetic is clearly necessary if one is to be justified in claiming that provision of an arithmetic model for any other set of axioms guarantees that they are free from formal contradiction.

Of the results discussed in the previous section it is perhaps Church's theorem rather than Gödel's which cuts deepest against the assumptions underlying Hilbert's original strategy. He had assumed that by making the rules of inference into formal, symbol manipulating rules it would be possible to distinguish provable from unprovable formulae by means of a simple notational characteristic. It was on this assumption that Hilbert's faith in the possibility of a finitary consistency proof was pinned. But Church's theorem shows that this is not possible for formulae in first order logic, and Gentzen and Chaitin gave further insight into this. With hindsight one can see that this might have been foreseen. Hilbert's grounds for insisting that arithmetic could not be reduced to logic were that essentially the same intuitions (successive construction of more complex symbols by application of recursive rules) ground our grasp both of finitary arithmetic and of a formal language such as PM. This is borne out in Skolem's proofs that every satisfiable wff of a first order language is denumerably satisfiable and is satisfiable in the domain of natural numbers. The proofs of these results rely essentially on regarding the formal language as a set of symbols over which the syntactic rules determine a structure which can then itself be used to provide an 'interpretation' (reflexive model) of the formal language. This means that a formal language capable of expressing arithmetic will itself be a potentially infinite structure which is at least as complex as that of the natural numbers. What the results of Löwenheim, Skolem, Gödel and Gentzen suggest is that whereas Hilbert was wrong in thinking that a meta-mathematical stance would allow a reduction of the infinite to the finite, in the form of a finitary consistency proof for a language containing quantification over an infinite domain, he was not wrong to think that it could effect a reduction. The reduction is of the non-denumerably infinite to the denumerably infinite.

We have already seen that the finitist–formalist position is unstable. Because formal languages are themselves potentially infinite, concepts such as formal consistency and provability, let alone completeness, already go beyond strict finitary meaningfulness. Many proofs, such as Gödel's completeness proof, which are necessary to give philosophic justifications for the position as originally motivated, do not stick to finitary methods. This suggests that at the very least a Hilbertian formalist cannot also be a strict finitist when it comes to either mathematics or meta-mathematics; the denumerably or potentially infinite must also be admitted as part of the irreducible base of arithmetic.

The positions which Gödel's theorems definitively rule out are the two reductivist options, the reduction of mathematics to logic and the reduction of full classical arithmetic to finitary arithmetic plus a formula game. It is far from clear that Hilbert seriously held the latter position although his 1927 piece on the foundations of mathematics contains remarks such as:

Mathematics proper becomes an inventory of formulas.

(p. 465)

Contentual inference is replaced by manipulation of signs according to rules; in this way the axiomatic method attains that reliability and perfection that it can and must reach if it is to become the basic instrument of all theoretical research.

(p. 467)

This formula game is carried out according to certain definite rules, in which the *technique of our thinking* is expressed.

125

These rules form a closed system that can be discovered and definitively stated.

(p. 475)

And the final outcome:

> mathematics is a presuppositionless science. To found it I do not need God, as does Kronecker, or the assumption of a special faculty of our understanding attuned to the principle of mathematical induction, as does Poincaré, or the primal intuition of Brouwer, or, finally, as do Russell and Whitehead, axioms of infinity, reducibility or completeness, which in fact are actual, contentual assumptions that cannot be compensated for by consistency proofs.

(p. 479)

The polemical tone of remarks such as these which occur in contexts where the strategy for providing an absolute consistency proof is made sufficiently precise to provide the starting point for mathematical investigation (the problem becomes sufficiently clearly posed for work to begin on trying to produce a solution to it, for it to become the foundation of a programme) is responsible both for Hilbert's reputation as a radical formalist and for the propagation of an image of mathematical reason as captured by the rules of a formal calculus; to reason is to do nothing more than to play a formula game. As with any ideology this has had both positive and negative effects. It provided the necessary ideological stimulus for work on what came to be known as Hilbert's Programme which included development of work in mathematical logic, the theory of formal systems, recursive function theory and computability. In mathematical terms, in terms of Hilbert's own criteria for mathematical problems, the story of the consistency problem is a success story. The problem comes to be sufficiently precisely posed for it to be possible to develop new mathematics which provides a solution – the required absolute consistency proof cannot be given. But the image of mathematical reason, the conception of mathematical activity which it fostered, has had negative effects within mathematics itself and beyond.

If mathematics is just a formula game then there is no point in demanding significance of mathematical work; just invent and play with formal systems. It is a recipe for a kind of freedom, a freedom from responsibility, which can create empty formalisms. If you think that that is all you should be doing, then that may very well be all you do. Outside of mathematics it has the effect of investing computers with the power of reason and of divesting reason of power to intervene in distinctively human affairs of ethics, politics and daily life. Reason bound by formal rules is tied within language, within culture, stands in opposition to freedom and creativity. Gödel's theorem was seen as a demonstration that the human mind is not a machine, was taken as proof of the limits of reason. Having put reason in formal chains it was now found to be impotent. Western philosophy as the way of reason, of logos, could be renunciated now that it had deconstructed itself. Hilbert should not, of course, be held responsible for the effects of his remarks. Even if he was a man of influence within mathematics his remarks would have had little impact if they had not been made to a receptive audience. Just how receptive may be gleaned from the extraordinary, proselytizing zeal of the papers of the early logical positivists (see Ayer 1959). Hilbert was speaking both with and to his time. Later disillusionment with the ways of reason can be understood as a reaction to such overoptimism, but the revolt fostered by disillusion was directed against reason seen in the image of it formalizing champions, not against the formal enchaining of reason.

If Hilbert was speaking with the voice of his time and if the remarks which were heard were those which were in accord with that positivist, anti-idealist spirit, it is doubtful whether it was his own voice. The remarks which were not heard, which were forgotten, do not accord well with this image. Hilbert the mathematician was far from thinking mathematics to be a mere formula game and was far from thinking that formal rules capture the essentials of mathematical reasoning. This can readily be seen by looking at other of his comments about mathematics and its foundations. But in an age of positivist enthusiasm, Hilbert's remarks about ideal elements were unlikely to be read in the idealist spirit which his repeated reference to Kant for an understanding of the role of ideal elements would warrant. There is a much more Kantian reading to be given to Hilbert's position, one which makes it a much more interesting philosophy of mathematics, if only because it does speak to the formalist–Platonist oscillation of working mathematicians. Mathematics is multilayered. The way it fits together is not that of reduction to a single system. It has a different sort of unity.

APPENDIX – RECURSIVE FUNCTIONS

Initial Functions: $Z(n) = 0$, $S(n) = n + 1$, $U_i^n(x_1 \ldots x_n) = x_i$,
where $1 \leqslant i \leqslant n$.

Schema of Primitive Recursion: $f(0,a) = p(a)$
$$f(n + 1,a) = q(f(n,a),n,a).$$

The *Primitive Recursive Functions* are all those which can be obtained from the initial functions by substitution or by application of the schema of primitive recursion.

μ-operator: If $g(x,y)$ is such that, for any x, there is a y such that $g(x,y) = 0$, then $\mu y(g(x,y) = 0)$ denotes the least y such that $g(x,y) = 0$.

The *Recursive Functions* are all those which are primitive recursive together with those which can be obtained by application of the μ-operator, i.e. by putting $f(x,y) = \mu y(g(x,y) = 0)$.

5

IDEAL ELEMENTS
AND RATIONAL IDEALS

The role that remains for the infinite to play is solely that of
an idea – if one means by an idea, in Kant's terminology, a
concept of reason which transcends all experience and which
completes the concrete as a totality – that of an idea which
we may unhesitatingly trust within the framework created by
our theory.

(Hilbert 1925 p. 201)

As we have said before, Hilbert was primarily a mathematician
and as a mathematician he was frequently impatient with philosophers. So although his concern for justifying mathematical
practice led him to make extended philosophical remarks concerning the nature of mathematics, these remarks do not amount to a
systematically articulated position. Some of his remarks suggest
the programme of attempting to reduce mathematics to a finitary
formula game. This had the advantage of reducing the philosophical problem to a problem assailable by mathematical methods. But
as Gödel showed, it thereby became susceptible to a negative
resolution; it can be proved that mathematics cannot be reduced to
a formula game. There are, however, other remarks made by
Hilbert which suggest a quite different picture of mathematics, one
not so amenable to precise mathematical formulation, but one
which may speak more directly to the experience of the working
mathematician and to the character of twentieth-century mathematics. This chapter will explore a way in which one might build
upon these suggestions to provide the basis of a philosophical
account of contemporary mathematics. It is not intended as an
exegesis of Hilbert's position, but uses elements of this position as
a starting point for developing an account of mathematical reason

as creative, the position Hilbert sought to vindicate by using finitary meta-theory. The demand for an absolute consistency proof carried out within the finitary meta-theory of a formal system of arithmetic was voiced in the context created by Frege, Russell and Peano of a reductive logicism and in the wider philosophical context of the rise of logical positivism. In this context Hilbert's formalism became assimilated to the reductive empiricist inspired logicism of Russell. In this form Hilbert's programme contributed to the formal enchaining of reason and the perception that mathematical reason would be legitimated only if it were shown *not* to be creative, i.e. only if it were shown that infinitary arithmetic is a *conservative* extension of finitary arithmetic. Gödel's incompleteness results tell against both formalist and logicist reductivist programmes, but just as these programmes have been elided so too have Gödel's two results. Usually reference is made only to Gödel's theorem. This assimilation of formalism to logicism, and vice versa, masks the strong differences between the attitudes toward mathematics, logic and reason adopted by Hilbert on the one hand and Frege or Russell on the other. Hilbert originally wanted to vindicate the creative problem solving power of reason, not to deny this power. He wished to justify the claim that proof of the consistency of a set of axioms for a mathematical theory is a demonstration of the existence of a mathematical domain of entities defined by those axioms. The impossibility of providing an absolute (finitary) consistency proof for arithmetic does not in and of itself demonstrate the untenability of the position Hilbert wished to secure by its means. It does mean that Hilbert's strategy for rebutting Frege's criticisms fails and hence that some alternative way of meeting those criticisms would be required.

FORMULAE, SYMBOLS AND FORMS

Hilbert's Programme interpreted formalism to be the view that non-finitary mathematical sentences are *just* formulae, just marks on paper, configurations of symbols, having no meaning other than that of being subject to the rules of the formula-game in which they occur. Since computers play formula-games in just this sense (are symbol manipulators) mathematical reason takes on a computational image and the authority and character of mathematics as a whole become, in the public mind, formed by requirements to submit to the authority of computer printouts and by an ambivalence toward computers. Computers are on the one hand mindless tools, which can be used, even exploited, for creative purposes, and on the other are invested with the sort of power and authority which implies (would in any other context imply) the presence of a very rational mind.

But if computers can be manipulators of purely formal symbols, causal mechanisms transforming one set of displayed or printed marks to another, it is far from clear that this is possible for a human being. In other words, the computational image of reason may be seriously misleading at this point, misleading us into thinking that the view of non-finitary mathematical sentences as *just* marks on paper, having no further meaning, is possible. It may be possible if we equate the reasoning processes of human beings with the operation of a present day digital computer. But since it is the possibility of a strict formalist attitude which lends plausibility to the computational image of reason in the first place, and then makes possible its more complete articulation, neither of these positions can lend conclusive support to the other. This is not, however, the place to enter into arguments about whether computers could ever think, or become rational agents, in the same sense as human beings. The point is simply that if we start from the conception of a rational agent as capable not only of conducting a train of reasoning according to rules but also of reflecting on its own activity and of modifying its own activity and/or rules in the light of that reflection (capable of acting in accordance with the conception of a rule), then, as will be argued below, the possibility of any strict formalist position disappears. So if computers could be rational agents in this sense, then they too would not be manipulating symbols in a manner which accords with the strict formalist account; they too would have transcended the computational image of reason.

The idea of a pure formal calculus, an uninterpreted notation, is that of a system generated by a set of rules for producing sequences of marks on paper, where it is possible to specify an algorithm which will determine whether any given sequence has or has not been produced in accordance with the rules. The rules impose structural constraints on sequences, their production and transformation. Any reflective rational agent, one which can not only obey rules, but which has the concept of a rule, norm or standard, will be able to engage in such a concrete mark producing activity aware that it has some of the characteristics of a game in that it is self-contained and governed by rules which mean that some of the sequence productions and transformations which are possible for the agent are allowed but others are not. Any rational agent following such rules will realize that the production of a particular sequence of marks (token) will be representative of all other productions issuing from the same sequence of rule applications (the same procedure of construction). That is, grasp of a generative rule together with recognition of its character already builds in an advance from concrete mark (token) production to the conception of a type of mark or sequence of marks. Because rules are repeatedly applicable they are already inherently general. Rules which are rules of production, construction, determine the character of the product (are constitutive) in just those ways which make it possible to tell from the product whether it was or was not constructed according to the rules. The kind of rules thought to characterize a formal system thus immediately traverse the gap between particular and universal, token and type. In this way concrete marks cannot remain without signification; they symbolically signify the types of which they are the tokens. Rules of this kind characterize a type of process and a type of structure as generated by those processes, a structure which can be characterized and known through reflection on an active participation in the production of symbols which signify beyond themselves.

It is this which makes meta-mathematics, proof theory etc. possible. Formal language and formal systems become objects of mathematical study. But as objects of study they are no less abstract than numbers, points or sets. Numerals are no less abstract than numbers. To ask whether '$0 = 1$' is provable within a particular formal system of arithmetic cannot be to ask whether the particular token inscription on the previous line can be so proved – it clearly was not; it is to ask whether the formula (type) is provable.

Any formal notation, and in particular any mathematical notation, when it comes with rules specifying combinatorial procedures for the formation and transformation of its symbols, generates its own internal interpretation as an abstract structure. The system of notation (i.e. symbols plus rules) itself generates and can be viewed as an abstract, algebraic structure. This occurs when, for example, one moves from a system of logic to its associated Lindenbaum algebra. This is the ontologizing power of sign systems; they generate spaces, structures within which to dream. Recognizing this will take us a long way toward understanding the sense in which Hilbert's claim that a consistency proof is sufficient to ensure mathematical existence could be justified. An inconsistent set of rules will not define a structure, will not result in a playable game. Within a standard logical framework an inconsistent set of rules (axioms) will result in no structure over the set of sentences since all sentences become provable. On the other hand, one should not forget the close interdependence between abstract structure and rules as one might if one were to mistake this appearance of referential content and the existence claims based on it for literal meaning, meaning conferred by reference to independently existing extra-linguistic items. The elements of such a structure are not independent items but are constituted solely by their location in a system, a structure. (One needs only to think here of the way in which the number system takes on a life of its own and of the different lives it lives in binary, decimal and duodecimal notations.) This is reflected in the care which Hilbert took to insist that consistency only entitles one to claim the existence of mathematical entities as ideal elements and to distinguish sharply between ideal elements and possible objects of experience. Such elements lack the 'self-subsistence' that Frege required of objects. Frege's concept–object distinction, with its unitary logical category of object which embraces both physical and abstract objects, does not allow him to countenance Hilbert's existence criterion.

However, there is more packed into the notion of an ideal element than simply being the abstract referent of a token in an arbitrarily constructed notation-game. Similarly there is a reading of what it means for mathematics or logic to be formal which does not amount to viewing mathematics or reasoning as the rule-governed manipulation of otherwise meaningless symbols. When rejecting Frege's reduction of arithmetic to logic, Hilbert says:

Material [contentual] logical deduction deceives us only when we form arbitrary abstract definitions, especially those which involve infinitely many objects. In such cases we have illegitimately used material [contentual] logical deduction; i.e. we have not paid sufficient attention to the procedures for its valid use. In recognizing that there are such preconditions that must be taken into account, we find ourselves in agreement with the philosophers, notably with Kant. Kant taught – and it is an integral part of his doctrine – that mathematics treats a subject matter which is given independently of logic.

(Hilbert 1925 pp. 191–2)

Hilbert is here appealing to two interrelated aspects of Kant's philosophy. The first is the view that there are conditions other than those of mere logical consistency which must be satisfied before a concept can be thought to apply to objects, and thus before reasoning involving that concept can be thought to concern objects. The second is the view that mathematics is concerned with the possible determination of forms of intuition (forms of representation of objects) which can themselves be constructed in pure imagination. These two doctrines are interrelated because the forms of intuition are the source of the additional conditions constraining the possible content of a concept. Thus Kant says:

A concept which contains a synthesis is to be regarded as empty and as not related to any object, if this synthesis does not belong to experience either as being derived from it, in which case it is an *empirical concept*, or as being an *a priori* condition upon which experience in general in its formal aspect rests, in which case it is a *pure concept*. In the latter case it still belongs to experience, inasmuch as its object is to be met with only in experience. For whence shall we derive the character of the possibility of an object which is thought through a synthetic *a priori* concept, if not from the synthesis which constitutes the form of empirical knowledge of objects?

(Kant 1929 A220, B267)

The force of this position becomes clear when Kant makes a remark bearing on the conceptual (logical) possibility of a non-Euclidean geometry.

Thus there is no contradiction in the concept of a figure which is enclosed within two straight lines, since the concept of two straight lines and their coming together contain no negation of a figure. The impossibility arises not from the concept in itself, but in connection with its construction in space, that is, from the conditions of space and of its determination. And since these contain *a priori* in themselves the form of experience in general, they have objective reality; that is, they apply to possible things.

(Kant 1929 A221, B268)

Part of Einstein's achievement was to show Kant wrong on precisely this point; in the explication of his relativity theories he showed that and how it is possible to supply the concepts of non-Euclidean geometries with an objective, empirical content by showing how to reform, or restructure, the space–time framework within which all events and physical objects must be located in order to count as part of the totality which is the physical universe. This involved conducting thought experiments, with, for example, space ships or trains travelling close to the speed of light, to determine what would, in principle, be the physical and hence possibly observable consequences of this restructuring.

From the fact that Kant was wrong about the possibility of supplying content to non-Euclidean geometry it does not follow that he was wrong either about the way in which conceptual, logical possibility is constrained by forms of intuition (representation of objects) or in his identification of possible determinations of forms of intuition as the subject matter of mathematics. However, it does mean that forms of intuition cannot be assumed to be uniquely determined or timelessly fixed. At the same time that he invokes Kant, Hilbert was reworking the foundations of geometry in such a way that alternative 'representation spaces' (forms of intuition) become more readily and systematically available. The claim would be that mathematics is formal in that its concern is with forms of representation and their possible determinations. It is not concerned with the matter or content of those representations.

Such a view of mathematics as formal is by no means novel; it can be traced back at least to Aristotle. When Aristotle is explaining the difference between mathematics and optics he says

While geometry investigates natural lines, but not qua natural, optics investigates mathematical lines, but not qua mathematical.

(Aristotle 1984: Bk II p. 331, 193b20–24)

The geometer is concerned with points, lines, surfaces, the shapes things may have and the relations between them but without considering how these are or may be materially realized. Aristotle, contra Plato, does not take this to imply that shapes exist independently of their material realizations. It is just that there are generalizations which can be made about the relations material things have or can have in virtue of their shapes and sizes, which do not depend on the material out of which they are made.

It is by reference to the Kantian variation on this Aristotelian distinction between form and matter that we can reinterpret Hilbert's remarks about numerals and geometrical diagrams, remarks which have customarily been taken to support a strict, computational kind of formalism. Reading the remarks in the light of the Kantian doctrines to which Hilbert alluded we get a version of a formalist philosophy of mathematics according to which mathematics is concerned with forms, not with Platonic forms, but with forms of representation of objects. Where Kant appeals to the construction of the objects of mathematics in imagination, Hilbert appeals to the production of marks on paper, to empirically constructed symbols.

> As a further precondition for using logical deduction and carrying out logical operations, something must be given in conception, viz., certain extralogical concrete objects which are intuited as directly experienced prior to all thinking. For logical deduction to be certain, we must be able to see every aspect of these objects, and their properties, differences, sequences and contiguities must be given, together with the objects themselves, as something which cannot be reduced to something else and which requires no reduction.... The subject matter of mathematics is, in accordance with this theory, the concrete symbols themselves whose structure is immediately clear and recognizable.
>
> (Hilbert 1925 p. 192)

As was argued above, if Hilbert really meant 'concrete symbols', the particular token inscriptions, then the position he is proposing would not make sense. Indeed the condition that for logical deduction to be certain we must be able to see every aspect of the symbols of which it is composed can never be fulfilled by concrete particulars. Part of what constitutes the independent reality of a physical object is precisely our lack of ability ever to claim complete knowledge of it, especially on the basis of simple inspection (what is the chemical composition, what are its dimensions to the nearest ten thousandth of an inch, when was it written etc.). As Kant makes plain, it is only of objects which we construct and which we regard as constituted solely by their method of construction that we could even hope to make this kind of claim. It was for this reason that in his *Critique of Pure Reason* he introduced pure imagination as the medium in which such entities can be constructed and presented as objects of knowledge. In the *Critique of Judgement*, however, he provides an account of symbolic reference which could serve as an alternative route to mathematical objects. The constructions we use may always be empirical, pencil and paper constructions of concrete symbols, but they are read as symbols, i.e. as representative of a construction which is not in any way materially conditioned and whose product is therefore constituted wholly by the method of construction, this abstraction being an inevitable accompaniment to the grasp of a method or rule of construction as just that, something which is repeatedly applicable and which generates entities having in common those characteristics which depend on the mode of construction.

> All *hypotyposis* ... or sensible illustration, is twofold. It is either *schematical*, when to a concept comprehended by the understanding the corresponding intuition is given, or it is *symbolical*. In the latter case, to a concept only thinkable by the reason, to which no sensible intuition can be adequate, an intuition is supplied with which accords a procedure of the judgement analogous to what it observes in schematism, i.e. merely analogous to the rule of this procedure, not to the intuition itself, consequently to the form of reflection merely and not to its content.

> All intuitions which we supply to concepts *a priori* are therefore either *schemata* or *symbols*, of which the former contain direct, the latter indirect, presentations of the concept. The former do this demonstratively; the latter by means of an analogy (for which we avail ourselves even of empirical intuitions) in which the judgement exercises a double function, first applying the concept to the object of sensible intuition, and then applying the mere rule of the reflection made upon that intuition to a quite different object of which the first is only the symbol.
>
> (Kant 1951 §59 pp. 197–8)

Kant protested against the logicians' tendency to oppose the symbolic to the intuitive. He insisted that the symbolic is a mode of the intuitive, in other words that symbols are a way of (re)presenting particulars. A symbol is not a mere mark devoid of representational function, but is a means of (re)presenting abstract particulars in such a way that we may be tempted to think of such things as having an independent existence, whereas in fact, according to Kant, they are projections of the rules we employ. It is here that the Kantian notion of an ideal element connects both with his account of symbols and with his view of mathematics as dependent upon the rational agent's ability to form the conception of a rule as well as to act in accordance with it.

IDEAL ELEMENTS AND IDEALS

Kant sharply distinguished mathematical reasoning from logical deduction. Mathematical reasoning is reasoning from the construction of concepts, whereas logical deduction is reasoning from concepts. The rules for constructing mathematical representations (numerals or diagrams) are simultaneously rules for constructing particulars and, in virtue of the generality inherent in all rules, give rise to concepts (the concept of an X as that which results from the construction C). Mathematical reasoning thus involves imagination and intuition in a way in which logical deduction does not, for mathematical reasoning characteristically starts from the construction of a particular (presentation and representation of an object and hence something which can only occur in empirical or pure intuition) and moves to a general concept and a general result. Reasoning from the construction of concepts is possible because what is grasped by reason is the principle, the method of construction. Only when this is grasped is it clear that there can be no end to the series of natural numbers.

But now the mind listens to the voice of reason which, for every given magnitude – even for those that can never be entirely apprehended, although (in sensible representation) they are judged as entirely given – requires totality. Reason consequently desires comprehension in one intuition, and so the [joint] *presentation* of all these members of a progressively increasing series. It does not even exempt the infinite (space and past time) from this requirement; it rather

138

renders it unavoidable to think the infinite (in the judgment of common reason) as *entirely given* (according to its totality).

(Kant 1951: §26 p. 93)

Our reason naturally exalts itself to modes of knowledge which so far transcend the bounds of experience that no given empirical object can ever co-incide with them, but which must nonetheless be recognized as having their own reality, and which are by no means mere fictions of the brain.

(Kant 1929: B71 pp. 310–11)

The number series as an actually infinite totality is an *ideal* element, i.e. an individual thing which is determined solely by an idea of reason. Ideal elements have no objective reality (are not part of the world of experience or of any independent reality transcending experience) but neither are they figments of a deranged imagination. Ideals supply reason with the standards it needs to employ in systematizing a domain of knowledge or a practice. It is reason which in imposing the demand for systematic unity presupposes an idea, that of the form of the whole of knowledge of a given kind, a whole which is prior to determinate knowledge of the parts and which contains the conditions that determine *a priori* the position of any given part in relation to the other parts. It is reason which, in setting cognitive ideals (standards), specifies what form the answers to our questions must take in order to count as answers, which postulates the form and location in relation to existing knowledge of the knowledge that we lack.

I understand by idea a necessary concept of reason to which no corresponding object can be given in sense experience. Thus the pure concepts of reason, now under consideration, are *transcendental* ideas. They are concepts of pure reason, in that they view all knowledge gained in experience as being determined through an absolute totality of conditions. They are not arbitrarily invented; they are imposed by the very nature of reason itself, and therefore stand in necessary relation to the whole employment of understanding.

(Kant 1929: A327, B384 pp. 318–19)

Ideals have no objective reality (independent existence). In other words, in order to engage in number theory we first have to project the completed series of numbers as the object of study through which the goal of our theoretical knowledge is specified. But this is merely a projected unity; it is not given as an object, but is hypothetically projected as the object of study. We conduct number theory *as if* the numbers formed a completed series because it is this which makes possible the systematization of arithmetical knowledge.

Since ideal elements are not possible objects of experience, they cannot be presented in empirical intuition, nor can they be constructed in imagination; they can only be symbolically represented. It is therefore possible to introduce a symbol which represents the totality of natural numbers, but its representative function is secured wholly by the role it plays in relation to representations of the finite numbers. There is no independent route, no more immediate way, of representing such an entity. It exists only as the projection of the concept of natural number, which in turn is a product of the rule for generating the natural number series taken together with the counting and calculating practices in which numbers are involved. When Cantor introduced ω as the first infinite ordinal number, the first number after all the natural numbers, he introduced it as a limit number, i.e. quite literally as that to which the number series points, but which it never attains – the ideal which is also a *focus imaginarius*.

Transcendent ideas ... have an indispensably necessary, regulative employment, namely, that of directing the understanding toward a certain goal upon which the routes marked out by all its rules converge, as upon their point of intersection. This point is indeed a mere idea, a *focus imaginarius*, from which, since it lies quite outside the bounds of possible experience, the concepts of the understanding do not in reality proceed; none the less it serves to give to these concepts the greatest [possible] unity combined with the greatest [possible] extension. Hence arises the illusion that the lines have their source in a real object lying outside the field of empirical knowledge – just as objects seen in a mirror are seen as behind it.

(Kant 1929: A644, B672, p. 533)

It is by shifting attention to centre on this *focus imaginarius* that Kant's philosophy transforms into Peircean pragmatism. For in the realm of the ideal Kant had already said:

The hypothetical employment of reason has, therefore, as its aim the systematic unity of the knowledge of understanding, and this unity is the *criterion of truth* of its rules.

(Kant 1929 A647, B675 p. 535)

The law of reason which requires us to seek for this unity, is a necessary law, since without it we should have no reason at all, and without reason no coherent employment of the understanding, and in the absence of this no sufficient criterion of empirical truth. In order, therefore, to secure an empirical criterion we have no option save to presuppose the systematic unity of nature as objectively valid and necessary.

(Kant 1929: A651, B679 p. 538)

In other words, coherence is, in this domain, the criterion of truth and it is only within the framework provided by the employment of the standard of coherence and systematic unity that it is possible to deploy an objective empirical criterion. It was to just such a standard of systematic unity that Einstein appealed when developing his theories of relativity – the idea that all laws of nature as laws governing a single reality should exhibit the same invariances under spatio-temporal transformations. The *focus imaginarius* is the conception of reality which guides enquiry, which makes possible the formulation and justification of explanatory ideals, conceptions of adequate proof or evidence, and in this way supplies the content for empirical notions of truth. But it is the projection of a demand for unity for which there is and can be no ultimate justification. The goal is not even fixed but changes as our cognitive ideals change. This is the respect in which a twentieth century pragmatism must depart from Kant. Reason itself does not have a sufficiently fixed, closed and unchanging nature for a once and for all knowledge of its ideals to be possible. This is nowhere more evident than in the development of mathematics over the past two centuries. The conception of mathematical reality has changed dramatically, as have styles of proof, along with methods and procedures for tackling problems. What neither Kant nor Hilbert sufficiently appreciated was that in the effort to impose systematic unity by making its own principles explicit reason does more than sharpen its focus, it actually reworks the image of reality at the *focus imaginarius*, which is but an artefact of the imaginative projection of forms of representations, forms which are themselves constituted by the rules of representational use.

GEOMETRY: DIAGRAMS AND RIGOUR

In Hilbert (1900) we find views on geometrical diagrams and the requirements of geometrical rigour which are more consonant with a Kantian reading of the symbolic function of mathematical symbols than are the remarks in the 1925 paper. Hilbert first firmly rejected the reduction of geometry to arithmetic (the elimination of geometric intuition) in the interests of rigour.

> While insisting on rigour in the proof as a requirement for a perfect solution of a problem, I should like, on the other hand, to oppose the opinion that only the concepts of analysis, or even those of arithmetic alone, are susceptible of a fully rigorous treatment. This opinion, occasionally advocated by eminent men, I consider entirely erroneous. Such a one-sided interpretation of the requirement of rigour would soon lead to the ignoring of all concepts arising from geometry, mechanics and physics, to a stoppage of the flow of new material from the outside world, and finally, indeed, as a last consequence, to the rejection of the ideas of the continuum and of irrational number. But what an important nerve, vital to mathematical science, would be cut by rooting out geometry and mathematical physics!
>
> (Hilbert 1900 pp. 78–9)

He then went on to outline his own conception of what is required for geometrical rigour.

> The use of geometrical symbols as a means of strict proof presupposes the exact knowledge and complete mastery of axioms which lie at the foundation of those figures; and in order that these geometrical figures may be incorporated in the geometrical treasure of mathematical symbols, a rigorous axiomatic investigation of their conceptual content is necessary. Just as in adding two numbers, one must place the digits under each other in the right order so that only the rules of calculation, i.e. the axioms of arithmetic, determine the correct use of the digits, so the use of geometrical symbols is determined by the axioms of geometrical concepts and their combinations.
>
> (Hilbert 1900 p. 79)

Thus geometrical symbols (diagrams and accompanying algebraic notations) do not fully determine their own symbolic interpretation. Many of the same diagrams and notations will be used in reasoning within both Euclidean and non-Euclidean frameworks. Here it is very clear that concrete tokens do not form the mathematical subject matter. It is the symbolic reference these acquire on being constituted as products of a representational system.

This conception might be further elaborated by viewing geometry as a mathematical study which arises out of pre-existing representational practices, practices of the diagrammatic representation of spatial characteristics and spatial relations, just as number theory, the mathematical study of numbers, arises out of practices of counting and calculation. Line and circle diagrams are used to represent and assist in reasoning about concrete physical situations (the layout of a building, the tiling of a floor, the construction of a bridge, finding the best route from A to B). Reasoning about the diagram is substituted for, or becomes reasoning about, the situation represented and thus forms of representation become constitutive of what is represented. As such practices arise its rules and standards will be implicit. Such reasoning is neither 'strict proof' nor has any degree of assured universality. The mathematical discipline 'geometry' can come into being only alongside the moves which 'create' its objects, i.e. make explicit the abstraction separating mathematical lines from physical lines, mathematical circles from physical circles. This occurs at the point when there is a move toward making the rules of reasoning explicit via an examination of the conceptual content of the symbols (diagrams). This amounts to an examination of the presuppositions built into the representational practice (which are necessary conditions of the possibility of that particular practice). For example, if one draws a square grid on which to work out the ground plan of a building thus

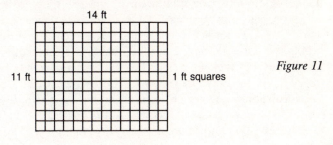

14 ft

11 ft   1 ft squares

Figure 11

then one will have presumed that the lines forming the grid have no thickness (one could not see them if this were actually so in the diagram). That is, one has presumed that the drawn lines symbolize mere divisions, mathematical lines with no thickness. Mathematical definitions of the basic components of spatial diagrams (point, line, plane, circle etc.) found in Euclid's *Elements* are definitions incorporating and systematizing such assumptions just as the axioms and postulates record and systematize further assumptions made in the representational practice. So, for example, the parallel postulate corresponds to the assumption that projection using straight lines perpendicular to a given straight line preserves lengths (distances).

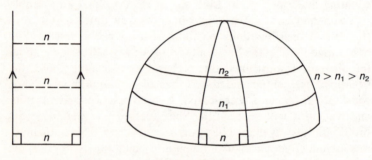

Figure 12

The abstract entities of geometrical theory are thus generated by the systematization of a representational practice and the co-ordinate pressure to treat diagrams both as representing physical situations and as symbolizing 'pure' mathematical constructs which are already 'ideal' forms. They are not encountered in perception, and could not be encountered as objects of perception, but they are nonetheless possible objects of experience in that they are part of the determinate representation of space – they are concepts which become constitutive of the world of experience as a spatial world (in Kant's terminology, they are constructed *a priori* in pure productive imagination), e.g. the equator is a mathematical line which is part of the empirical world. But it is a demand of reason, the demand to order, to systematize, to rigorize which compels this idealization and which gives diagrams their two readings – makes them point in two directions, to the physical world they are used to represent and to the mathematical entities they symbolize

144

(c.f. p. 1). This same move confers universality on diagrams and on mathematical reasoning carried out by their means.

When introduced to the notion of geometric proof we are schooled to read a diagram as a merely illustrative, heuristic device because we are not trying to prove a result about the particular drawn figure but about the class triangular objects or areas that this diagram could be used to represent. The triangle

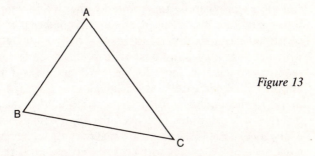

Figure 13

is an image which is therefore read symbolically as referring to an abstract mathematical form and yet it is crucial to geometric reasoning that it be focussed on a particular triangle (the universal is found in the particular) because it is only to particular triangles that construction lines can be added etc. The reasoning is that of the construction of diagrammatic representations in which one diagram can have repeated representational uses and where a procedure of construction can yield multiple equivalent representations. It is a procedure of construction that can be carried out non-materially (since material is irrelevant to it) in pure imagination.

Hilbert, modifying Kant slightly, interpolates geometrical diagrams between material objects and their mathematical representations. The intuitions on which theoretical geometry is founded are those derived from the practice of drawing diagrams to represent spatial, structural characteristics of material objects. This representational practice already ignores the material (does not represent material characteristics) and preserves only the spatial. Yet, as Kant argues, such representations become constitutive of material objects as we think of them (represent them to ourselves and in our discourse) in that we do think of them as having determinate (mathematically precise) shapes. If we identify an object as a square tile, we attribute to it the geometrical properties of a square without investigating in more detail the extent to which it deviates from the perfect square. In this way the formal characteristics of representational practice are constitutive not only of the representations of objects but also of the objects as represented. Objects are never known in themselves, but only as represented in some way or other. But, as we have seen, it is at this point necessary to depart from Kant on two related counts. The successful application of non-Euclidean geometry shows that the empirical world can be represented within spatio-temporal forms whose structure is not Euclidean, and this makes it easier to raise questions about the extent to which strictly mathematical forms structure everyday intuitions. If in ordinary life we are neither required to choose, nor do we have the basis for choosing, between Euclidean and non-Euclidean geometry, then neither of them, to the mathematical exactness required to manifest their divergence, constitutes (provides the representational form for) everyday experience. This means that formal, mathematical knowledge cannot claim the sort of authority *vis-à-vis* the empirical world that it once could; it must return to its association with the art of reasoning rather than with the science of the fabric of the world. This is to say that Kant gives a misplaced empirical reality to geometrical forms: they too should have been seen as forming part of the *focus imaginarius* – the projected vision of a reality which transcends, or lies behind, the world of everyday experience. On the other hand this does not invalidate the general account of the association between mathematics and forms of representation as an account which promises to explain the two faced (pure–applied) character of mathematics in such a way as to cast light on both its epistemology and ontology.

Geometry requires a move from the construction of diagrams (particular empirical representations of empirical situations) to the universal (form) via a method of construction (schema). At the same time it imposes a secondary (esoteric, symbolic) reading on the diagram (a reference to a non-empirical ideal). It involves reasoning from construction of a particular to a general method of construction which becomes definitive of the universal. This is the move which Kant elsewhere terms reflective judgement. It is a move in which reason legislates to itself in the formation of ideals. (It is also the move which falls under the Peircean notion of abduction, although Peirce's notion has a wider range of application.)

Judgment in general is the faculty of thinking the particular under the universal (the rule, the principle, the law). If the universal is given, the judgment which subsumes the particular under it ... is *determinant*. But if only the particular is given for which the universal has to be found, the judgment is merely *reflective*.

(Kant 1951 p. 15)

The reflective judgment, which is obliged to ascend from the particular in nature to the universal requires on that account a principle that it cannot borrow from experience, because its function is to establish the unity of all empirical principles under higher ones, and hence to establish the possibility of their systematic subordination. *Such a transcendental principle, then, the reflective judgment can only give as a law from and to itself.*

(Kant 1951 p. 16; my italics)

PRAGMATISM, AXIOMATIZATION AND IDEALS

What does it take to establish the possibility of a systematic subordination of one body of principles under a higher one? The formulation of general principles which provide such a systematic subordination, such as the axiomatic presentation of a system incorporating 'ideal elements'? Establishing this possibility and establishing the existence of the ideal elements are one and the same task since the ideal elements provide the figurative focus for the systematization; they are an integral part of the form of representation which orders and systematizes. This would provide the basis for a response to Frege's objection (see pp. 98–9) that the only way to show a set of axioms to be consistent is to show that they express truths about an independently existing domain of objects; consistency cannot entail existence because one cannot move from the existence of an idea or a concept to the existence of an object conforming to the idea, or falling under that concept. Clearly Frege would be in the right if ideal elements were Platonic Forms, existing wholly idependently of human beings, their reasoning and representations. But this is not the kind of existence claimed by Hilbert, on a Kantian reading of the notion of an ideal element. The existence claimed is wholly co-ordinate with demonstrating the possibility of a kind of systematic order by the provision of a form of representation which embodies it. Forms of representation cannot themselves be arbitrarily invented. They have to work. They have to serve the purposes for which they were created. They have to resolve antecedent problems, by rendering perspicuous some of that which was previously obscure. They have to cohere with as well as extend other accepted forms.

Hilbert treated axiomatization as the answer to a demand for increased rigour in mathematics. Axiomatization systematizes and unifies pre-existing practices of representation and of reasoning conducted on these representations. The demand to impose this kind of order is a demand of reason, it is a demand for order, for logical clarity and precision. It is constrained by the intuitive understanding embedded in the practices, but not necessarily determined by these. (This is clearly demonstrated by the very different directions in which, for example, Reimann, Cayley, Poincaré and Hilbert sought to systematize post-Euclidean geometry.) Rigorization has a legislative force – to legitimate and justify where possible, but also to clarify the standards for justified practice in such a way that violations can be clearly discerned. It is a process in which familiar concepts are reforged, rather than one in which eternal truths are intuited.

Hilbert's own axiomatization of Euclidean geometry legitimates and makes it possible to rigorize the practices of analytic geometry where algebraic and geometric representations are combined, where geometric conclusions are based on algebraic reasoning. But by providing this axiomatization Hilbert altered the symbolic reading of geometrical diagrams. When he says that the axioms determine the meaning of 'point', 'line' and 'plane' it is not the axioms alone – since the axioms make precise the rules for reasoning from diagrams they establish what it is that the diagrams are to be read as symbolizing. The same diagrams may be used when working within either a Euclidean or a non-Euclidean geometry where the meanings of 'point', 'line' and 'plane' will be different in that the diagrams must be interpreted differently. If axiomatization determines how geometrical figures are to be read (symbolically) it legislates this reading. Definitions of the figures appearing in diagrams must be couched in the terms which are primitive in the axioms. Thus Hilbert's axiomatization of geometry also requires redefinition of basic geometrical concepts. In other words, geometrical objects as the symbolic referents of diagrams must be rethought from the axioms via the diagrams; the axioms alone cannot determine these referents, but neither can the diagrams. Such a reading cannot be merely conceptual nor can figures conforming to these rationally imposed conditions be constructed in the imagination. They can be imagined only indeterminately; it is the point at which reason pushes imagination beyond its empirical limits, where they conspire to transcend the empirical and the humanly constructible. The three-dimensional point continuum of Hilbert's Euclidean space is an abstract representation space, indeterminately and problematically posited as the realm within which geometrical representations can be constructed. It is a form, or a framework capable of organizing, by being imposed on, or supplied with empirical content. But unlike the Kantian forms of intuition it does not necessarily structure all experience; rather it is a framework which can be deployed to organize either the whole of space or merely limited domains.

By changing the symbolic reference of geometrical diagrams, Hilbert's axiomatization simultaneously changed the concept of space (it becomes natural to talk of *a* space) and extended its domain of application. Any domain of discrete entities may form a space if they satisfy the conditions laid down in the axioms, in which case all the representational and reasoning techniques of geometry may be applied in that domain. In other words, the rigorization of practices of geometrical representation and reasoning itself modifies those practices, changes the geometrical concepts and the geometer's world (his projected reality). The work of Hilbert and others opened the way to a more abstract notion of space – a Hilbert space – which is used, for example, to provide the mathematical framework for more recent formulations of quantum mechanics. The justification for such a move can only be that of the coherence and utility of the whole body of the reasoning and representational practices it inaugurates and facilitates.

A space as an actually infinite totality of points is, for Hilbert, an ideal element. Thus symbols signifying such things have no meaning beyond what is given by the rules of their use. But if we have come down the Kantian road to this point we see that this cannot mean that such symbols are devoid of content – are mere marks on paper. An ideal element is not produced as the symbolic referent of an arbitrary, self-contained symbol-game. Rather it arises from rational standards either consciously imposed on or already implicit in a representational practice. It is an imaginative presentation of the goal or object of the practice, a presentation which takes on the guise of a particular (object) as the standard by reference to which success is judged. In the case of mathematics, then, formalism will not, in advocating the introduction of ideal elements, admit the arbitrary introduction of sets of axioms to be taken as definitive of the primitive terms they employ. Rather, any proposed axiomatization and any introduction of ideal elements must be conducted on the ground of rigorizing, or bringing order to, an aspect of existing mathematical practice, of unifying and systematizing its procedures. Ideal elements will be the product of completions or totalizations of operations which allow a new systematic unity to emerge. 0, negative numbers, $\sqrt{(-1)}$, the point at infinity, ω are all ideal elements of this kind. The introduction of such elements is legitimate to the extent that they genuinely do complete, bring new order into the practices into which they are introduced. That is, if defined axiomatically, not only must the axioms be formally consistent but their consequences must be consistent with what was provable prior to the introduction of the ideal elements. If 0 and $\sqrt{(-1)}$ make possible the extension of the number system then they must not disrupt the pre-existing core of that system. Rules for their use must not allow '1 = 2' to become provable.

This does not, however, mean that such extensions have to be conservative, i.e. that every statement about the old numbers provable by their means should be provable by direct means, i.e. without them. If we think of the introduction of ideal elements as being itself justified by requirements of rigour, systematization and unification then they will be most fully justified if, by their means, it is possible to prove general principles concerning the old numbers which would not have been provable otherwise. In other words, if the conception of an infinite totality of natural numbers is merely a rational projection, a *focus imaginarius*, then the thought that the truth values of all statements about the natural numbers is fixed and determined independently of the methods of proof we develop is also a regulative principle, a rational ideal only. To require conservative extension for ideal elements is to be taken in by the illusion presented by a rational ideal. This is perhaps another way of reaching the conclusion to which Dummett (1963) argues. The lesson which he wishes to draw from Gödel's theorem is that there is an inherent vagueness in the conception of the totality of natural numbers because there is no possibility of closure either in regard to what counts as a proof of a proposition concerning all natural numbers or in regard to the definable properties of natural numbers. To interpret Gödel's first theorem as demonstrating the existence, for any formal system of arithmetic, of an arithmetic truth which is not provable in that system is to assume the system consistent and to assume that we are in posession of a perfectly determinate conception of the natural numbers as a domain forming a model for the formal system and in which every statement in the language of that system is either true or false. This is to forget that our grasp on that domain is given only by our understanding of the Peano axioms and the use of numerical induction as the means by which theorems concerning the totality of natural numbers can be proved. In other words it is to be taken in by the illusion created by a regulative ideal.

Hilbert seems clearly to recognize the regulative character of the assumption that the truth values of mathematical statements are determinate. In his frequently repeated 'no *ignorabimus*' slogan

> This conviction of the solvability of every mathematical problem is a powerful incentive to the worker. We hear within us the perpetual call: There is the problem. Seek its solution. You can find it by pure reason, for in mathematics there is no *ignorabimus*.
>
> (Hilbert 1900 p. 81)

he makes it clear that one of the ways in which a problem may be 'solved' is by proving that a solution is impossible. So for example he cites the old problems of proving the axiom of parallels, squaring the circle, as having finally found fully satisfactory and rigorous solutions, although not in the originally intended sense. It has been shown that they could not be solved as originally posed, but we now see why they could not be solved.

Yet to a greater extent than perhaps Hilbert himself was willing to acknowledge, the introduction of ideal elements does not leave the pre-existing domain fixed. The conception of number as the measure of a magnitude is what militates against the admission of either 0 or negative numbers as numbers. If they are admitted as ideal elements, to complete the system, then they have no interpretation as proper numbers (magnitudes). But as they come to form a single representation system with the positive numbers, they come to have applications. The result is that the concept of number itself is no longer tied to that of magnitude. In this sense even the finitary significance of numbers has not, historically, been

151

without change. Peano's axiomatization of the natural number system, making it essentially a system of entities generated from 0 by repeated application of the successor operation, again opens up a pathway to the field of recursive function theory, the theory of algorithms and the whole modern computational life of the number system. Computation as understood by this route is not what it was before those developments. Moreover, as Russell pointed out (see pp. 74–5), the axiomatization has the consequence that arithmetic can be applied to (the formal axioms will have as a model) any infinite progression. In such a model arithmetical operations such as addition and multiplication may have no natural significance. This widening of the potential application for numbers (which is not new to the extent that cryptographers, cabalists and other mathematical mystics traded on just this possibility for generations) means that the number system can be treated simply as an exemplar of a certain kind of structure and hence as a medium within which it is possible to prove results holding for all such structures and having implications for things quite other than numbers, measurements or discrete quantities. But as the device of gödel-numbering illustrates, it becomes possible to use this process in reverse. To start with a non-arithmetic structure and show that it is possible to build an arithmetical model (analogue) of it and by this means define arithmetic predicates which would not naturally have arisen just by thinking about numbers (for example the predicate of numbers which corresponds to their being the gödel-number of a provable arithmetic formula). In other words there is a complicated dialectic between internal symbolic readings of numerals (as referring to natural numbers) and external model-theoretic/semantic specifications of reference for them as entities of some other kind, where there is feedback between these as regards proof procedures and definition of concepts. What emerges is not a static picture of a set of entities on the one hand with a determinate and fixed set of reasoning procedures which can, once and for all, be characterized and certified as reliable.

Hilbert's shift to meta-mathematics and to proof theory looked at first sight as if it might yield an absolute consistency proof because it seemed to involve stepping outside the realm of mathematical abstraction and back into that of empirical reality. Yet, as was argued above, if proofs are themselves to be made the object of mathematical study they too are abstract objects.

Moreover, as soon as we form the concept of a formal system of arithmetic and presume that it either is or is not consistent we have already introduced a new ideal element, one on a par with the totality of natural numbers. To assume that the formula which expresses $1 = 2$ either is or is not provable in a given formal system is to assume something of the form '$\exists x\ R(x,a)$ v $\neg\exists x\ R(x,a)$' where x ranges over a potentially infinite domain, and hence where '$\exists x\ R(x,a)$' is not finitarily significant. From the purely finitary stance, then, one has no right to assume at the outset that a formal system either is or is not consistent; to do so is to introduce an infinitary assumption. This becomes even clearer in the light of gödel-numbering when the concept of provability has to be expressed by quantification over the natural numbers, i.e. by the very ideal element whose introduction is in question. What gödel-numbering highlights (by exploiting) is the fact that the natural number series (in its modern guise) is the form of representation for the products of all discrete, finite and sequential constructive operations. By shifting to proof theory one does not step outside the realm to which this form applies. One may very well, however, by focussing on procedures of computation and proof be able to prove things about the natural numbers that could not be proved directly, or which may only subsequently be provided with a direct proof. But so far as consistency goes, the most that can be demanded is internal coherence. This is essentially what Gentzen's consistency proof provides.

Does this legitmate the actually infinite? Could it be used to underwrite a Platonist view of mathematics? Clearly not. The criterion of legitimation is one acceptable to a pragmatist, but not to a realist. Nevertheless one would need to enquire further concerning what it is that a demonstration of coherence achieves with respect to use of the law of excluded middle in association with quantification over an infinite totality, such as that of the natural numbers series, if it is not a proof of the independent existence of this totality. Essentially what Hilbert sought was legitimation for a procedure, not for a factual assumption. He sought to legitimate the mathematician's claim to the right to reason as if the numbers formed an independent totality. He sought legitimation for the symbolic mathematical projection of a realm which surpasses the sensible and which does not have the same status as the empirical realm; it is a realm in which it is possible to think imaginatively and creatively about possible forms of representation of the empirical realm. It is a conception which guides the mathematician's activity by suggesting that his problems do have solutions. Yet as a conception of an object which provides of a standard of truth it is illusory, since it is a product of rational standards, not their source.

LOGIC AND THE OBJECTS OF MATHEMATICAL KNOWLEDGE

The notion of an 'ideal element' was introduced to mark a sharp distinction between knowledge of empirical reality and purported knowledge of a super-sensible or transcendent reality. Frege makes no such distinction. For Frege all objects, whether mathematical or empirical, are on the same logical footing and in being so are presumed to be covered by the same conceptions of truth and knowledge. Knowledge of mathematical objects is treated by analogy with knowledge of empirical objects with the consequence that mathematical objects can no more be defined into existence than empirical objects. The mathematician is likened to the geographer exploring unknown territory. This is the analogy which both Brouwer and Hilbert, taking their cues from Kant, rejected.

Whereas Kantian intuitions play many of the roles of Fregean objects by virtue of being particular, unlike objects they are not self-subsistent. Intuitions, whether empirical, or pure, are subject to the forms of intuition (space and time); empirical intuitions are the material of experience; they are phenomena or appearances, they are not things in themselves. This means that Kant can require as an additional condition on the applicability of a concept that it must be shown not merely that it contain no contradiction, but also that it be shown that something falling under it would be a possible object of experience, i.e. that in pure intuition it is possible to specify a method (schema) for generating a spatio-temporally structured image of such a thing. (For example if the mathematics of relativity theory suggests the concept of a black hole, the existence of such a thing can only be taken seriously as a physical consequence of the theory, rather than an artefact of the mathematics, if it is possible to specify what would count as observational evidence for the existence of one.) This condition is required only to the extent that we want to secure objective employment for our concepts (use them in the expression of empirical knowledge). If we try to employ concepts – such as 'substance' (self-subsistent individual) and 'cause' – beyond the realm of what is given in space and time, we use them without justification and the resulting propositions cannot pretend to the status of knowledge of an independently existing realm (knowledge which is objective in the sense of being knowledge of independently existing objects).

It is by reference to this doctrine that both Hilbert and Brouwer can appeal to Kant to justify the division they make between finitary and non-finitary mathematics. Frege had dismissed Kant's account of arithmetic on the explicit ground that arithmetic applies without restriction to all objects of thought, not only to what is given in sense perception. But (as was argued in Chapter 2) this is to overlook the fact that Kant counts objects of thought amongst intuitions. Brouwer and Hilbert resurrect Kant's account of arithmetic precisely by building on the fact that it is not restricted to sensory intuition, but can apply to all thought constructs. For Brouwer mathematics concerns the form of all thought considered as the thought of an empirical subject, thought which is developed in time, i.e. in a finite linear sequence. He ignored Kant's account of geometry, taking this to have been discredited.

Since Hilbert's proof theory arises from insisting that one should look on the process of mathematical proof as the process of constructing finite symbolic structures, carried out by beings who are temporally and intellectually finite, his conception of elementary arithmetic and of proof theory has marked similarities with that advocated by intuitionist mathematicians. The objects of finitary mathematics can be constructed in intuition, via the empirical construction of symbols. Since we are incapable of carrying out infinite constructions, there is no determinate intuition which could be supplied for an infinite totality or for the result of repeating an operation infinitely many times. The lesson which Brouwer and the intuitionists drew from this was that there can be no significance attached to assertions concerning actual, completed infinites. Mathematics can only meaningfully talk about the finite and the potentially infinite, that which is always actually finite, but always incomplete. Our understanding of the potentially infinite is grounded in our grasp of constructive operations (such as adding 1) which can be indefinitely repeated. Unrestricted use of the law of the excluded middle, when talking about infinite series, is therefore illegitimate because it presumes that it makes sense to think of the series as completed; it involves assimilating the infinite to the finite. Mathematics, as a discipline claiming the status of objective knowledge, cannot therefore treat of the infinite other than via the principles for the construction of potentially infinite series, and must be rebuilt in such a way that this restriction is acknowledged. In a precisely similar vein Kant had demanded that philosophy abandon traditional (dogmatic) metaphysics which employs the notions of substance and cause beyond the bounds of possible experience and had himself argued that at the limits of experience the law of the excluded middle and the use of non-constructive proofs (proofs of positive propositions which proceed by showing that their negation leads to a contradiction) should not be allowed (Kant 1929: A789, B817 and A794). In this respect the intuitionists are re-imposing some of Arnauld's demands: Arnauld's critique of Euclidean rigour is paralleled by the intuitionist critique, grounded in an account of human cognitive capacities, of Frege's re-imposition of those standards.

Hilbert came to a different conclusion, but one which still respects the limitation of objective knowledge claims to the domain of possible experience. His move is in effect to urge that it is a mistake to assimilate mathematics too closely to empirical science. The goal of theoretical mathematics is not to claim objective knowledge in the sense of knowledge of objects whose existence is independent of us in the way in which empirical objects are independent of us. The initial subject matter, that of finitary mathematics, is given through construction. Since there can be no infinite construction, mathematical concepts which appear to take us beyond the finite cannot be treated in the same way as finitary concepts. Judgements using them can have no content; since there can be no intuition (matter) supplied for such concepts, such judgements are purely formal and can concern only forms of representation. But can there legitimately be judgements transcending the finite? Kant not only allowed for this, but thought it inevitable. Mathematical reasoning as reasoning from the *construction* of concepts is possible because what is grasped by reason is the principle, the method of construction. Only when this is grasped is it clear that there can be no end to the series of natural numbers. But it is practical reason which pushes us beyond the finite. It is the recognition of reasoning as an activity conducted according to rules, of reason as placing demands of rigour, order and justification, and of the operation of reflective judgment on these activities as introducing totalizations, ideas and ideals. Such understanding as is acquired in this way bears on rational representational practices; it is not knowledge of a transcendental reality.

Here there is a conception of rigour and of the role of axiomatization which departs fundamentally from assumptions which were held in common between Euclid, Arnauld and Frege – in particular the assumption that there is a uniquely correct axiomatization which reflects the 'true' rational order, whether this be mind-dependent or mind-independent, and that axioms are self-evident truths. Even though Arnauld stressed the art of reasoning, he presumed that the order he imposed on his ideas, on the basis of criteria of clarity and distinctness, reflected an objective order amongst the things represented by those ideas. I.e. he, like Descartes, supposed that mathematical reason is a route to theoretical knowledge descriptive of an objective reality. This is the conception which Kant's transcendental idealism worked to undermine; practical reason and the reflective judgments to which it gives rise do not yield knowlede of objects but understanding of the rational subject and of the forms imposed by its practices. These considerations suggest that the divergence between the logicist's conception of reason and Hilbert's formalist conception of mathematical reason runs deeper than previously indicated. This divergence is reflected in the difference between their attitudes to logic and the relation between pure and applied mathematics.

For Russell and Frege formal logic provides the rational framework for all assertoric discourse. Logic was to provide the framework for an ideal language of science. This required that (i) the relation between pure mathematics and its applications must be displayed within this framework and thus that it be represented as a matter of the logical deduction of particular instances from a general theory, and (ii) that all reasoning be displayed as taking place within language and thus as concerned with the relation between descriptive statements. Hilbert tacity rejected this conception of the role of logic. Implicit in his disagreement with Frege over axiomatization is his lack of acceptance of the view of logic as the framework for a universal language. His conception of logic is descended from logicians such as Boole and De Morgan; it is that of logic as a calculus, something closely akin to arithmetic because it shares its mathematical character and mode of application.

Both Boole and De Morgan developed an algebra of classes

where operations on classes are treated by analogy with operations of addition, subtraction and multiplication of numbers. If A and B are two classes A + B would be their union, A − B would be the intersection of A with the complement of B, and A.B would be their intersection. Logical priciples are then derived from basic assumptions, expressed as equations, concerning these operations. The logical equivalence of 'No A are B' and 'No B are A', for example, is immediate once 'No A are B' is expressed by the equation 'A.B = 0', if the commutativity of class intersection, expressed by 'A.B = B.A' is assumed. Both Boole and De Morgan noted the formal similarity between algebraic formulations of class logic and of propositional logic. Principles of class logic could, by interpreting letters as standing for propositions, 'A + B' as 'A or B', 'A.B' as 'A and B', 'A − B' as 'A and not B', be read as principles of propositional logic. In this way the basic assumptions about operations came to be seen as definitive of a kind of structure (a Boolean algebra) and logic results from the interpretation of an equation calculus which has potentially many interpretations.

From this standpoint there would indeed be no philosophical mileage to be gained by trying to 'reduce' arithmetic to logic. But if formal logic has the status only of a regionally and strategically deployed calculus, (i) it cannot be supposed to exhaust the principles of reasoning, and (ii) it does not display its own mode of application and the relation between pure mathematics, or formal logic, and its applications will not be a straightforward, logically formalizable relation. Further, since Hilbert talks about reasoning with geometrical diagrams and numerals it is clear that he presumes that mathematical reasoning does not always take place within language but may go via non-descriptive, non-linguistic representations.

These differences over logic, reason and the mechanisms of theory application are crucial to the disagreement between Frege and Hilbert concerning the role of axioms. They emerge at the level of logic over readings of the universal quantifier and at the level of mathematics over the relations between axioms, theory and application. In applying an arithmetic formula such as '7 × 3 = 21' the context of application determines what are the units being counted and hence what proposition the applied formula expresses, or what information is gleaned from it. It might be a question of calculating the number of sheets of paper required for seven copies of a three-page set of notes, or the area of a wall to be tiled. Similarly it will be context that determines the universe of discourse and the predicates involved in any application of the logical principle $\forall x \; (F(x) \lor \neg F(x))$. The universal quantifier does not range over all possible objects, but over those under consideration in the given context. On this view logical laws do not express universal truths, or determinate thoughts in Frege's sense. They are formulae, schemata, whose application involves specification of the domain over which any quantifiers are to range. Russell had already felt pressure to move some way in this direction and responded by introducing his type hierarchies. Here he presumes that every predicate (propositional function) carries with it, as part of its sense, an internal specification of the domain over which it is defined (its range of significance). Yet he found that this makes it impossible to state the principles of logic or arithmetic in such a way that they retain the strictly universal applicability that was the original motivation for Frege's logicist programme. These principles, Russell had to say, are typically ambiguous; they apply throughout the type hierarchies but can only actually be stated for each level separately. When logic is viewed as a calculus, however, its principles do not have to be stated using universal quantifiers; they do not express logical truths but rules of inference whose use is co-ordinate with representing the domain to which they are applied as having a certain kind of structure. This difference was emphasized by Gentzen's presentation of logic as a system of natural deduction rather than as an axiom system.

What difference does this make? Is it not always possible for a universe of discourse to be explicitly specified? If so universal quantification over objects can be read as ranging over *all* objects and talk about all of a specific kind is rendered by using expressions of the form $\forall x(K(x) \rightarrow \ldots)$ (cf. Quine 1960: Chapter 5). There are at least two reasons why Hilbert should have resisted this argument. (i) It presupposes that a predicate can always be given to delimit a universe of discourse, i.e. that for any domain there are necessary and sufficient conditions specifiable which mark off this domain from other domains of objects. But this is the demand for complete definition of concepts which Frege made, which Russell had partially to retract, and which Hilbert regarded as the fatal mistake, the one which opened Frege's system up to Russell's paradox (Hilbert 1904 p. 130). (ii) Hilbert did not regard the universe of legitimate discourse as closed or given in advance. With the advance of mathematics new entities are added to its domain. To treat the universe of objects as determinate is to tie logic to metaphysical assumptions whether of a Platonist, or, as in Russell's case, empiricist nature. (Note that this is explicit in Quine's slogan 'To be is to be the value of a bound variable' (Quine 1948). But Hilbert's aim was precisely to free mathematics from such assumptions. Indeed, Hilbert argues (1904 p. 135) that one can talk of the elements of a set only after the set itself has been introduced. In other words, in the context of an axiomatic development of a theory, determination of the range of variables (those for points, lines and planes, for example) is not and cannot be extensional since the range is determined only through axioms which employ quantification over it. If quantification were here read extensionally the implicit definitions provided by axiom systems would indeed violate all Russell's strictures against impredicative and viciously circular definitions. Russell's reductionist programme, which treated mathematical objects as logical fictions (rather than ideal elements), relied heavily on use of extensional readings of quantifiers. But for Hilbert Russell's 'constructions' are one and all 'ideal' because they involve quantification over infinite domains. From Hilbert's point of view, Russell's proposed solution to his paradox, even if it had delivered technically, was not a philosophically adequate solution. Equally, from Russell's point of view, admitting a creative role for reason in its representation of the empirical world would render objective knowledge impossible; the sterility of reason was a necessary condition of its objectivity. It is this conception of objectivity as requiring undistorted representation of an independently existing reality which is tacitly rejected by Hilbert. When he insists that quantification over an infinite domain of mathematical objects is not to be read as quantification over a domain of pre-existing objects, that the domain of quantification is given only subsequent to the axioms which define it and that this is necessary if paradoxes are to be avoided, this is tantamount to suggesting that the mathematical realist's conception of objectivity is at the root of the paradoxes. It is in this respect that the rigorous implementation of axiomatic method is viewed as providing an alternative solution to the problems created for the foundations of mathematics by the set theoretic paradoxes. Hilbert further comments that if new primitive notions are added, extending the system (e.g. negative numbers are added to the positive integers) then the previous axioms will thereby have their scope enlarged and must be suitably modified. He was well aware that this conflicted with Frege's view that axioms should express truths about an antecedently existing domain and that definitions could serve only to abbreviate complex identifications of pre-existing objects or concepts.

But is it possible to take Hilbert's position seriously and admit the legitimacy of impredicative specifications of mathematical domains? Clearly if one is working within the framework supplied by logicism and by its concept of the way axioms express truths, then this is not possible. However, as argued above, the conception of logic as a calculus does not sanction such a view of axioms. To see what view it does lead to we might return again to Hilbert's axiomatization of geometry.

The real numbers provide a model for Hilbert's axiomatization of Euclidean geometry in the sense that they are a domain of objects over which relations are defined which can be used to interpret the primitive terms in the axioms in such a way that the axioms so interpreted are true of the real numbers. On the other hand there is also a sense in which n-dimensional Euclidean space can provide a model for any set of n independently variable physical magnitudes (dimensions), such as time, mass, velocity, charge etc. These can be represented by spatial dimensions and their possible relations modelled by geometrical structures, on which geometrical reasoning is conducted whilst being interpreted as reasoning about the relations of physical magnitudes. The latter is the situation in which geometry and geometrical reasoning is applied and the former is a situation is which the theory of real numbers is used to gain information about (by providing an arithmetic model of) geometrical relations, geometric axioms. It also serves to legitimate moves in analysis which depend on the ability to move between geometric and numerical representations. Both of these situations can be represented as situations in which the geometric axioms are supplied with a model by being interpreted over a given, externally specified domain of entities.

This was how Russell wished to view the matter and, with the development of close associations between model theory, semantics and logic, it has come to be seen as the standard view. The advantage, from Russell's point of view, was that it reduced pure geometry to a set of logically true, universally quantified conditional statements of the form 'for any domain D, if axioms A are true in D, then ...' and geometrical activity reduces to the derivation of logical consequences from axioms. There is no pure 'space' to be the object of mathematical knowledge. The disadvantage is that this conception of the activity of the pure-mathematician/geometer accords ill with mathematical experience and cannot in any case be applied to the activity in which Hilbert engaged when seeking a new and more rigorous axiomatization of Euclidean geometry.

What should, however, be noted is that the situations referred to above are, importantly asymmetric. In one case geometry is providing the 'space' within which the modelling is done. In the other the real numbers provide the ingredients for the model. The modelling situation requires a certain logical symmetry (at least a homomorphism between the structures) so that translation can go from model to modelled and back again. But this logical symmetry does not entail an epistemological symmetry. Models are constructed for the purpose of making a complex situation more tractable, for representing in a different, and hopefully more perspicuous way a situation which poses certain problems or about which one wants further information. Mathematical theories can be seen as theories of classes of models (or structures) – theories of forms of representation (as is made explicit in category theory). This serves to emphasize that not all representation is linguistic-descriptive. Mathematics does not apply by describing, but by modelling (picturing in a highly schematic way), substituting a simplified model within which, or on which, it is possible to conduct reasoning as a substitute for reasoning directly about the situation modelled.

Frequently the problem of how to bring the laws of an abstract, mathematically expressed physical theory to bear on actual cases lies in seeing how to represent the case in such a way that the laws, and the mathematical reasoning that goes with them, can get a grip on it. The procedure of modelling is familiar from, for example, elementary mechanics where ladders are represented first as rigid rods and then as straight lines, where a pendulum is represented as a point mass swinging on the end of a torsionless, inelastic string represented by a straight line, and so on. Reasoning is initially conducted on these simplified, mathematically tractable models. The process of reasoning on schematic mathematical representations of levers and balances made it possible and natural for Archimedes to use the modelling relation in reverse, thinking about trying to 'balance' two areas about a point on a straight line (see p. 11) as a means of calculating the areas of segments of curves. To calculate these areas he had to find a means of comparing them with the areas of triangles, since he can readily compute the area of a triangle from the lengths of its sides. Ptolemy constructed geometrical models of the motion of each of the planets using circles and supposing all circular motion to be uniform in part because he wanted to be able to predict their observed positions and to do this he had to represent their motions in such a way that the limited mathematical techniques available to him could be applied to yield the predictions. This required construction of a model out of components whose mathematical properties were well known. This kind of modelling requires imagination and ingenuity. It is also constrained by the purposes the model is designed to serve and by the sort of familiarity with available mathematical techniques that makes it possible to judge what kind of representation will be both appropriate and mathematically tractable. Just as a graphic artist or a sculptor must know his medium, its strengths and limitations, so a mathematical physicist must be familiar with the 'representation spaces' available in mathematics and their characteristic strengths and limitations as representational media. In this respect mathematics stands on the boundary between representational art and discursive reason. Mathematical reasoning is a species of artistic reason exploring and pushing to the limits its own representational forms.

But if mathematical theories are to provide model building resources they have to be more than formal systems. They have to have their own domains – intended interpretations. On pp. 144–6 it was suggested that it is the symbolic reading of geometric diagrams as constrained by the axioms which supplies their intended interpretation. In other words, it would be a mistake to seek for the intended interpretation amongst the class of externally specified possible models of the axioms. The intended interpretation requires a non-extensional reading of the universal quantifier; its domain is impredicatively and therefore indeterminately specified. It is a domain in which the axioms play a constitutive role in setting standards of truth and falsity. It is not a domain where truths independent of the axioms (neither provable nor refutable on their basis) exist, awaiting discovery. On the other hand, an indeterminately specified domain is one which is open to further determination.

If we can allow that mathematics is driven by problems, rather than by a quest for descriptive knowledge, then this openness to further determination may be seen as a virtue and a source of power rather than as a scandal and a source of scepticism. The criteria for determining whether a problem has been solved are not identical with those for determining when a descriptive statement is true or false. As Hilbert indicated, a problem, such as that of squaring the circle (or deciding the continuum hypothesis), may be solved either by giving a straightforward positive solution (inventing a procedure, providing a proof or a refutation from existing axioms) or by showing that it cannot be solved by the methods presumed at the time the problem was posed. In the latter case the problem may just be dropped (as with squaring the circle) or it may be reformulated and reposed as a somewhat different problem, as when one asks whether there are grounds from elsewhere in mathematics for determining an answer to the Continuum Hypothesis.

Frequently the solution to a problem is achieved by representing the problem situation in a new way, e.g. algebraically instead of geometrically, or by showing that it is closely related to another problem in another area, one which might be easier to solve. Mathematical reasoning as centred round problem solving is far from exhausted by logical deduction. The creative part of the reasoning is that of constructing the problem representation to which either calculation or deduction may then be applied to yield a resolution (the part that Descartes called 'analysis'). If a problem is solved by reasoning within an axiomatic system which introduces a novel concept or an ideal element what one requires is some assurance that this is a genuine solution, i.e. that alternative representations of the problem would yield the same result. This requires that a newly proposed system be consistent with other, already existing techniques on domains to which they can both be applied. It does not require assurance of some absolute reliability, for this does not make much sense in the context either of problem solution or forms of representation once one has discarded the thought that there are uniquely privileged, undistorting forms of representation. If any form of representation (e.g. that of a standard motoring map) represents only an aspect of something which may receive alternative representations, then reasoning on any representation can, if it does not remain aware of the limitations of its perspective (aiming to indicate roads, mileage etc. but not topography), become unreliable. For this reason the continued critical demand of constructivists, such as Bishop, that the meaning or significance of a problem, statement or question be specified is a necessary reminder.

Bishop (1973) argues that when a contemporary mathematician takes refuge in formalism, saying that meaning can only be understood in the context of the entire set of assumptions and techniques at his command, he inverts the natural order. The natural order, he says, would be to determine meaning first and then to base assumptions and techniques on the rock of meaning. To acquiesce wholly to Bishop's demands would be to lose sight of the way in which mathematical meaning is symbolically determined and thus of the very framework of projected ideals in which mathematical questions can be posed and presumed resoluble. However, he is correct to point out that this classical framework underspecifies 'meaning' (in that its referents are indeterminate) and that it fails to acknowledge this underspecification. If the classical mathematician assumes that a precise content is secured for a non-constructive existence proof, that he can bestow all the determinacy of an empirical or a finitely constructed object on the entity whose existence is proved, then he is taken in by the illusion of the projection of the rational demands of his practices. Bishop and the constructivists can rightly call for a more complete determination by constructive methods. These will yield more information than non-constructive ones, but they can never be wholly self-sufficient. The comprehension of their constructive character invokes classical totalizations. The dialectical relation between construction and formal systematization is what demands recognition and exploration.

Formalisms divorced from their epistemological roots can readily become over-extended, and thereby empty and unreliable. The effect of introducing a purely formalist spirit into mathematics is in tune with post-modern moves to discard unitary, hegemonic rational order in favour of a play of diverse perspectives. If there is not at the same time a recognition of the constraints placed by the notion of an ideal element as something introduced as a demand of reason, serving the purposes of unifying and systematizing, of bringing a new order into a domain, and thus also recognition of the significance of the domain so ordered, this will remain an empty play. Reason may be self-legislating, but it is, in mathematics, legislating to some purpose. Where this purpose is forgotten or ignored, then the result is just a game without external reference and without connection to the main areas of mathematics. Newly introduced 'ideal' elements do not become respectable mathematical entities merely by being postulated within an axiomatic framework. They have to prove their mathematical worth by making possible the solution of problems posed independently of them and recognized as genuine mathematical problems. At the same time their relation to already recognized mathematics is thereby established.

> Mathematics is good if it enriches the subject, if it opens up new vistas, if it solves old problems, if it fills gaps, fitting snugly and satisfyingly into what is already known, or if it forges new links between previously unconnected parts of the subject. It is bad if it is trivial, overelaborate, or lacks any definable mathematical purpose or direction. It is pure if its *methods* are pure – that is, if it doesn't cheat and tackle one problem while pretending to tackle another, and if there are no gaping holes in its logic. It is applied if it leads to *useful* insights outside mathematics. By these criteria, today's mathematics contains as high a proportion of good work as at any other period, and as any other area; and much of it manages to be both pure and applied at the same time.
>
> (Stewart 1987 p. 233)

LACK OF CLOSURE AND THE POWER OF REASON

As Bachelard had already noted in 1928, and reiterated in 1934, the rational spirit of contemporary mathematics (and hence also of contemporary science) does not have the closed character decried in post-modern critiques of reason. Bachelard's observation was based on a study of the 'revolutionary' developments which marked the transition from nineteenth- to twentieth-century physics – the advent of relativity theory and quantum mechanics – and the prior developments in mathematics which were a condition of their possibility – the development of non-Euclidean geometries, tensor calculus, Fourier analysis etc. These developments displaced the rational framework of classical Newtonian science, whose stability had seemed to underwrite the supposition that its form was uniquely required by reason. Reflection upon this transition results in more than the displacement of one rational

166

framework by another; it leads to recognition that there is no one representational framework which is uniquely required by reason. It leads to recognition of the possibility of there being justified revisions of forms of representation and of ways of reasoning, and thus to the idea of reasoning as a dynamic process in which frameworks are constructed and revised. Reason can no longer be thought to be determined by a static closed framework within which all reasoning must take place and by reference to which all justifications must be given. Both the logicist and formalist programmes illustrate the 'revolutionary' institution of new rational frameworks, even whilst they both continue to operate with the conception of a unique, closed rational framework. They are of interest as examples which serve to support Bachelard's view, for, as we have seen, the particular kinds of closures they envisioned cannot be achieved.

Frege's work, for example, undermines the Kantian presupposition of a reason closed upon and transparent to itself. In effect Frege's extension of logic, which rests on extending the mathematical notion of a function, constitutes a rejection (i) of Kant's separation between forms of judgment and forms of intuition (representation) and (ii) of the Kantian view of logic and reason as fixed and immutable, a feature on which Kant relied for his claim that a complete and exhaustive critique of pure reason was possible. Frege's work demonstrates the need to reject (i) and (ii) even as it explicitly adheres to the assumption of a closed reason and engages in the project of outlining a logic covering all possible forms of judgment. His work demonstrates the historical lack of closure of forms of judgment in that the mathematical notion of a function, on which he drew so heavily for his notation, for his distinction between concept and object and for his account of the quantifiers, first began to emerge only in the seventeenth century. In this way he unintentionally demonstrated the capacity mathematics has for introducing new forms of judgment, thus showing that forms of representation interconnect with forms of judgment in a more complicated and more dynamic manner than Kant had ever envisioned.

Hilbert's Programme set in motion moves to achieve a final closure of reason with computational chains. Gödel's incompleteness theorems show that complete computational closure is not possible. This was achieved by generalizing computational methods through the use of gödel-numbering and the concept of a recursive function. Here the reflexive, meta-mathematical use of computational methods, by which the Programme proposed to achieve computational closure, is used to demonstrate precisely the opposite – that such closure is not impossible. The possibility of re-interpreting numerals and formulae as referring to numerals and formulae instead of to numbers and statements about numbers generates a sort of feedback loop where consistency requires undecidability.

Now this same phenomenon can be made to appear not only for the formal language of a mathematical system, but also for a text written in a natural language. If words are presumed to have meaning only in virtue of their place in a linguistic structure, then the words of a text can legitimately be interpreted into any other words that sustain the same structure of inter-relations. Neither in the case of a formal system, nor in the case of a text viewed formalistically, is it possible to distinguish one uniquely correct, intended interpretation amongst the externally specified models, interpretations or readings. This would seem to be the insight underlying many of Derrida's arguments to the effect that there can be no 'correct' interpretation of a literary text. 'Organized by a code, even an unknown and non-linguistic one, [a piece of writing] is constituted in its identity as a mark by its iterability [i.e. by its having a repeatable structure] (Derrida 1977 p. 180). From this situation Derrida has drawn the conclusion that the attempt at interpretation is to be abandoned in favour of 'reading'; that the use of reason to arrive at and provide a defence of an interpretation is impossible (see Eldridge 1985). Similarly, formalists in the philosophy of mathematics advocate abandoning the concept of mathematical knowledge and with it the epistemological role of reason in mathematics.

However, the phenomenon of re-interpretation, of multiple application of a formalism, which is exploited in Gödel's incompleteness theorems to demonstrate the lack of closure of mathematical reason, is also the source of the representational power of mathematical forms. It is what is required for arithmetic to have multiple and diverse applications. Moreover, as we have seen (pp. 147–54), unforeseen applications play an important role in the development of mathematics. I have also argued (pp. 130–3) that even in the case of mathematical formalisms, it is not possible to adopt a purely formalist stance, a stance which will prohibit one from making sense of the notion of an intended interpretation.

The formalist stance is possible only if marks on paper, 'words', are isolated from all reference to users. When this is done, it does indeed make no sense to talk of interpretation, intended or otherwise. But as soon as these marks are treated as items which have a use and which have been used, then we know where to start looking for an interpretation – not to the private intentions of a specific user (the author), but to the practices within which this specific use occurred. (The contribution of practice and cultural context (form of life) to the interpretation even of inscriptions designated as part of a system of formal logic is brilliantly demonstrated by Scott 1970.) This will not lead us, even in the case of mathematical formalisms, to interpretations which are wholly precise and free of ambiguity, i.e. not to the sort of interpretations required by referential semantics, for the lack of rational closure within mathematical practice that allows for multiple applications will, at the level of reference to mathematical entities, be reflected as indeterminacy. But indeterminacies within an 'intended' interpretation are not, except for dogmatic referential realists, ground for thinking that there is no such interpretation at all. The words of a natural language lead a more complex life than mathematical symbols and this renders the process of interpretation more complex, subject to more indeterminacies, but not theoretically impossible.

In mathematics the story does not stop at Gödel's theorem. Computers are in the process of dismantling the very image of reason which generated them. (Constructs may be used to deconstruct their own image.)

(a) By their means complex new representational forms (programmes) are constructed. A complex piece of software, such as the Unix operating system, may have been compiled, modified and added to by a number of different people no one of whom now fully understands the whole programme in detail. It does not follow from the fact that such programmes are human constructs, supplied with humanly formulated rules, that they are thereby readily understandable or predictable. Complex programmes present us with a reality with which we have to deal, and where the notions of correct and incorrect understanding still make sense. But this reality is not of the same order as physical reality. Computer programmes are not natural phenomena, nor are they artifacts whose behaviour is governed by natural laws, even though they are dependent on such physical artifacts for their implementation and exploration.

(b) By exploiting the computational and representational powers of computers, unsuspected features of old mathematical forms have been discovered. For example, when the equation for a parabola, $y = kx(1 - x)$, was treated as a recursive function, $f(n + 1) = kf(n)(1 - f(n))$, and successive values were plotted, unexpected patterns were revealed. Different initial values and different values of the parameter k were found to yield strikingly different forms of behaviour. For $k = 2$, $x_0 = 0.9$, a fixed point (steady state) of 0.5 is reached at x_7. For $k > 3$, various kinds of periodicity emerge. For $k > 3.58$ the mapping becomes 'chaotic'. (See Stewart 1989 pp. 155–61.) On a suitably programmed computer the value for k can be adjusted and the effect of the adjustment visually displayed. In this way computers make possible a much more concrete, because readily manipulable, representation of mathematical entities, illustrating the respects in which mathematical reasoning is a form of rational poiesis. The fields of chaos theory and fractal geometry are new branches of mathematics which depend heavily on computational power and on the possibility of translating the results of calculation into visual displays. 'Fractal geometry is a new language. Once you can speak it, you can describe the shape of a cloud as precisely as an architect can describe a house' (Barnsley 1988 p. 1).

Part of the novelty of fractal geometry is that it challenges long held assumptions about the sort of structure which can be rationally comprehended, for example, the assumption that such a structure must have simple atomic components, or starting points, from which it is built up in a finite number of steps. Fractal structures are infinitely complex; there is complexity 'all the way down'. Successive magnifications of a section of a fractal curve reveal similar structures nested within each other indefinitely (they are 'self-similar'), just as successive magnifications of a perfectly straight line reveal smaller and smaller perfectly straight line segments. Fractal geometry includes deterministic geometry, which not only extends our ability to characterize complex spatial structures but also to represent complex dynamical systems the behaviour of whose parts is governed by deterministic laws. The resulting models have begun to effect a radical change in the way people think about complex deterministic systems (see Gleick 1987, Briggs and Peat 1990, and Prigogine and Stengers 1984). This capacity to develop new representational forms whose application brings in its wake new ways of thinking and reasoning illustrates the sense in which mathematical reason does not form a closed and fixed system, but is something which has always the potential for development in new directions. The lack of closure of classical analysis is a precondition of the possibility of finding new ways of investigating old forms, such as the equation for a parabola. This does require re-interpreting the equation, linking it to computation in new ways, but not in such a way as to break with, or lose sight of, older interpretations.

Fractal geometry and chaos theory are still in the exploratory stage. At this stage, where there is no axiomatic theory, where much exploration is quasi-empirical, where rigorous proofs for many claims are lacking, is it very hard to adopt a formalist stance (unless one wishes to dismiss it as not part of mathematics), since there is no formal system as yet. The situation is analogous to that which faced Descartes with the development of analytic geometry and it exhibits the kind of constructive, intuitive, creative use of reason which led Descartes to reject formal logic out of hand. But post-modernism, taking its cues from Derrida, tends to run Cartesian intuitive and constructive reason, which is reliant on the capacity of critical reflection (Kant's judgment), together with discursive, logically structured, linguistic and mechanizable reason. Both together are condemned under the sign of the western tradition's 'logocentrism', under which reason is identified with the logic of identity. This however, is to ignore the mathematical turn away from Euclidean standards of rigour (see Chapter 1). Undeniably there are unresolved tensions within the Cartesian conception of reason, tensions between dynamic and static, between method and intuition, between epistemology and metaphysics. But it is possible to argue (see Lachterman 1989) that the Cartesian rejection of logic, the turn toward a new method based on new mathematical methods which emphasize construction and inventive discovery over demonstrative proof, marks a fundamental shift which was crucial to the 'modern' attitude. This attitude was not founded on the logic of identity or on a traditional Aristotelian metaphysics of substance, but on attempts to dispense with them. It marked a shift away from the verbal and conceptual rational plane of a purely speculative and contemplative philosophy, toward a philosophy of rational practice in which method yields knowledge which will in turn have practical application in the reconstruction of man's material and social environment. The essentially modern belief in progress required an epistemological dynamism and a dynamic conception of human reason, even when it was set, problematically, in the framework of a closed and totalizing metaphysics. It was Kant who displaced metaphysics, turning its totalizations into regulative ideals of human practice. To ignore the shift toward method, toward construction and the practical, the shift away from the verbal and discursive, is to leave no space within which to make sense of the logicist demand for a return to Euclidean standards of rigour or of the resistance of twentieth century mathematics to those demands. It also makes it appear that the only alternative to the closed, computational reason of logicists and formalists is a wholesale rejection of the tradition of rational enquiry.

However, it was neither Frege nor Russell who set the tone for twentieth-century mathematics, but Hilbert, who, with his advocacy of axiomatization rather than logical reduction as the embodiment of mathematical rigour, sought to defend the openness of mathematics to creative determination. Foundationalist attempts to secure absolute guarantees for the use of mathematical reasoning by rendering it calculatory, mechanical and closed were thwarted by mathematics itself. It is true, as we have seen above (pp. 156–7) that Descartes, Arnauld, Frege, Kant and Russell shared presuppositions which have been abandoned in the wake of developments prompted by non-Euclidean geometry and Hilbert's Programme. Axiomatization and rigorization no longer aim at a unique, 'true' rational order or aspire to capture 'Truth' with the certitude of self-evidence. But this does not mean that demands for consistency and coherence, rigour and rational order have been abandoned. The very effort to axiomatize and systematize, to impose rational order is itself a force for change through the complex interplay between the internal symbolic readings of pure theory and the external, model theoretic interpretations of application (see pp. 148–52). The boundaries between these are fluid. These findings are in accord with Derrida's statement:

> I believe that every conceptual breakthrough amounts to transforming, that is to deforming, an accredited, authorized relationship between a word and a concept, between a trope and what one had every interest to consider to be an unshiftable primary sense, a proper, literal or current usage.
>
> (Derrida 1983 pp. 40–1)

and also with Wittgenstein

> the proof changes the grammar of our language, changes our concepts. It makes new connections, and it creates the concept of these connections. (It does not establish that they are; they do not exist until it makes them.)
>
> (Wittgenstein 1956 II.31 p. 79)

If reason were confined to the logic of identity it could clearly not yield such changes, could not be the route by which we make the breakthrough which amounts to a shifting of the conceptual sands. This is why Wittgenstein's comment is far more radical, outrages more sensibilities, than Derrida's. How can a proof (a logical structure) be a proof and at the same time change our concepts? Well, maybe not all proofs are logical structures; maybe even mathematical proofs which seem to have logical structures should not be identified with those structures. The debates about what exactly is proved by Gödel's theorem suggest that we cannot equate what the proof proves with the last line of the formal proof. The older term 'demonstration' carries with it the idea that a demonstration is that by means of which we are shown something, something which might amount to a conceptual breakthrough. I have argued that just this kind of shifting will inevitably be the product of drives toward axiomatization and rigorization – drives which seek to implement rational ideals.

Deconstruction exploits the necessary instabilities, the inevitable lack of closure of conceptual systems. But the necessity of a lack of closure, openness to deconstruction is itself not universal. Only systems internally recognizing the force of rational ideals are subject to this sort of destabilization. In the absence of those ideals the exposure of undecidabilities or of incoherences, has no force. In this light the flight to a post-modern proliferation, its restriction of analyses to the fragmentary and the perspectival, through abandonment of standards of coherence and consistency and the demand for rational order, is itself a continuance of the quest for security, for a defence against the possibility of radical critique, the kind of critique which is a force for change and development. In this way the postmodern position readily slides into the conservative strategy of liberal pluralism which, by allowing a place for all, needs to listen to the claims of none (Donoghue 1983). It is the strategy of the classical mathematician's retreat to formalism when he admits the respectability of intuitionist and constructive mathematics as alternative formal systems, worth investigating, but which thereby not only deprives their proponents of any critical voice, but also insulates itself from their critique, and so effects a form of rational closure.

To give up on ideals is, as Derrida allows, to have 'strategy without any finality', the 'strategy of someone who admits that he does not know where he is going'.

> I should like it to be also like a headlong flight straight toward the end, a joyous self-contradiction, a disarmed desire, that is something very old and very cunning, but which also has just been born and which delights in being without defence.

> (Derrida 1983 p. 50)

Recognition of the indeterminacies present even within mathematics, for centuries the paradigmatically rational discipline should not entail abandonment of ideals of reason, ideals of coherence and consistency. The illusion of closure is a product of failing to distinguish the ideal from the real, a failure to recognize the purely regulative function of the ideal. But once this is recognized, the indeterminacies in mathematical representations, the undecidabilities in any formal system, signalling the discipline's lack of closure, can be seen to be its source of problem solving and creative power, not a sign of weakness or of imperfection. Indeterminacies are loci of potential creative determination and the very mechanisms responsible for indeterminacies are those which confer superior representational power. Mathematical constructions are both concrete and symbolic; they do not provide an escape from representation to reality but serve as a reminder that representations are part of human reality just as human reality is constructed by representations. Mathematical reason may not provide access to a super-sensible realm of absolute forms, but it has the capacity to refuse any totalizing entrapment by 'objectifying' the totalization, and thereby destabilizing it. This is the lesson to be learnt from the story of the foundations of mathematics from the paradoxes of Cantor and Russell to the theorems of Gödel.

GLOSSARY OF SYMBOLS

$\neg p$	it is not the case that p.
$p \,\&\, q$	p and q.
$p \vee q$	p or q.
$p \rightarrow q$	If p then q.
$p \equiv q$	p if and only if q (p is materially equivalent to q).
$p \equiv_{df} q$	p is, by definition, equivalent to q.
$\forall x \, A(x)$	for every x, $A(x)$.
$\exists x \, A(x)$	there is an x, such that $A(x)$.
$\exists_1 x A(x)$	there is exactly one x such that $A(x)$.
$a =_{df} b$	a is, by definition, identical with b.
$A \vdash B$	B is deducible from A.
iff	if and only if.
wff	well-formed formula.
$x \in y$	x is a member of the set y.
$x \notin y$	x is not a member of the set y.
$x \neq y$	x is not identical to y.
ω	omega, the first infinite ordinal number.
$\aleph_0$	aleph zero, the first infinite cardinal number.

FURTHER READING

1 AXIOMATIZATION, RIGOUR AND REASON

Some of the issues raised here concerning the 'modern' conception of reason are discussed in much greater historical depth by Lachterman (1989). Hacking (1973) contrasts Descartes' intuitive conception of reason with Leibniz' much more formal, discursive conception. Gaukroger (1989) gives a fuller account of Descartes' conception of inference and its internal tensions. By far the most sensitive discussion I have read of the contrast between Greek, seventeenth century and late nineteenth century conceptions of rigour is by Gardies (1984).

2 FREGE: ARITHMETIC AS LOGIC

Dummett (1967) remains one of the best brief introductions to Frege's philosophy. Resnik (1980) locates Frege's philosophy of mathematics in a wider philosophical context and includes discussion of Frege's arguments with Hilbert over the axiomatization of geometry. Tragasser (1984) is an excellent exposition of a Husserlian approach to the philosophy of mathematics, the kind of approach which Frege rejected as psychologistic.

3 RUSSELL: MATHEMATICS AS LOGIC

Chihara (1973) provides a readily accessible and sympathetic account of Russell's position. Gödel (1944) illustrates how, on a realist reading, the Axiom of Reducibility undermines the whole edifice of the ramified type hierarchy. The introduction and first chapter of Wang (1986) relate Russell's philosophy of mathematics to the wider context of empiricism and logical positivism. The whole book is an extremely interesting reflection on the development of analytic philosophy in the first half of this century and on the role which logic and the philosophy of mathematics played in that development.

176

4 HILBERT: MATHEMATICS AS A FORMULA GAME?

Although there are many expositions of Gödel's theorem I find the long way round through Hofstadter (1979) to be one of the most successful in terms of being both understandable and conceptually sound. It is also useful because it illustrates the many-facetedness of the issues raised by Gödel's techniques and by his results; they do not only concern formal systems of arithmetic. An alternative, equally inventive and successful but very different approach is that of Smullyan (1987). Stewart (1987) contains a brief account of Chaitin's work. Shankar (1988b) develops an interesting critique of artificial intelligence research by revealing its roots in the formalism of logical positivist interpretations of Hilbert's Programme. Conway (1976), who explores connections between number and games, illustrates the point that even if calculation were a form of game, number theory would not thereby reduce to the mere manipulation of formal symbols.

5 IDEAL ELEMENTS AND RATIONAL IDEALS

Deleuze (1984) provides a brilliantly brief and readable exposition of Kant's philosophy of the faculties, and my reading of Kant has been influenced by this. I am also drawing on the epistemological framework provided by Bachelard (as explicated in Tiles (1984)) and especially on Bachelard (1928). Nerlich (1976) and van Fraasen (1970) are good introductions to the philosophical problems posed by nineteenth century developments in geometry. Poster (1989) contains a balanced discussion of the conflicting claims of critical theory on the one hand and post-structuralism on the other.

BIBLIOGRAPHY

Anellis, I. H. (1989) 'Distortions and discontinuities of mathematical progress: A matter of style, a matter of luck, a matter of time ... a matter of fact', *Philosophica* 43, 163–96.

Archimedes (1897) *The Works of Archimedes*, ed. T. L. Heath, Cambridge University Press, Cambridge.

Archimedes (1912) *The Method of Archimedes Recently Discovered by Heiberg: A Supplement of the Works of Archimedes, 1897*, ed. T. L. Heath, Cambridge University Press, Cambridge.

Aristotle (1975) *Aristotle's Posterior Analytics*, trans. J. Barnes, Clarendon Press, Oxford.

Aristotle (1984) *Physics* in J. Barnes (ed.) *The Complete Works of Aristotle*, revised Oxford translation, Princeton University Press, Princeton, N.J.

Arnauld, A. (1964) *The Art of Thinking*, trans. J. Dickoff and P. James, Bobbs-Merrill, Indianapolis, IN.

Ayer, A. J. (1959) (ed.) *Logical Positivism*, Free Press, Macmillan, New York.

Bachelard, G. (1928) *Essai sur la connaissance approchée*, Libraire Philosophique, J. Vrin, Paris.

Bachelard, G. (1934) *Le nouvel ésprit scientifique*, Presses Universitaires de France, Paris. Translated as *The New Scientific Spirit* by A. Goldhammer, Beacon Press, Boston, (1984).

Barnsley, M. (1988) *Fractals Everywhere*, Academic Press, San Diego, CA.

Benacerraf, P. and Putnam, H. (1964) (ed.) *The Philosophy of Mathematics: Selected Readings*, Prentice-Hall, Englewood Cliffs, NJ.

Benacerraf, P. and Putnam, H. (1983) (ed.) *The Philosophy of Mathematics: Selected Readings*, 2nd edn, Cambridge University Press, Cambridge.

Bishop, E. (1985) 'Schizophrenia in contemporary mathematics' in M. Rosenblatt (ed.) *Erett Bishop: Reflections on Him and His Research*, AMS, Providence, RI, pp. 1–32.

Bostock, D. (1974) *Logic and Arithmetic*, Vol. I: *Natural Numbers*, Oxford University Press, Oxford.

Bostock, D. (1979) *Logic and Arithmetic*, Vol. II: *Rational and Irrational Numbers*, Oxford University Press, Oxford.

Briggs, J. and Peat, F. (1990) *Turbulent Mirror*, Harper & Row, New York.

Brouwer, J. (1912) 'Intuitionism and formalism' in Benacerraf and Putnam (1964) and (1983).

Cantor, G. (1955) *Contributions to the Founding of the Theory of Transfinite Numbers (1895, 1897)*, trans. P. E. B. Jourdain, Dover, New York (Originally published Open Court, La Salle, Ill, 1915).

Chaitin, G. (1987) *Algorithmic Information Theory*, Cambridge University Press, New York.

Chaitin, G. (1988) 'Randomness in arithmetic', *Scientific American* 259(1), 80–5.

Chihara, C. (1973) *Ontology and the Vicious Circle Principle*, Cornell University Press, Ithaca, NY, and London.

Church, A. (1936a) 'A note on the Entscheidungsproblem', *Journal of Symbolic Logic* 1, reprinted in Davis (1965).

Church, A. (1936b) 'An unsolvable problem of elementary number theory', *American Journal of Mathematics* 58, 345–63, reprinted in Davis (1965).

Conway, J. H. (1976) *On Numbers and Games*, Academic Press, London, New York, San Francisco.

Davis, M. (1965) *The Undecidable*, Raven Press, Hewlett, New York

Dedekind, R. (1963) *Essays on the Theory of Numbers (1872)*, trans. W. W. Beman, Dover, New York (Originally published Open Court, La Salle, Ill, 1901).

Dee, J. (1570) *Mathematical Preface to the Elements of Geometrie of the most auncient Philosopher EUCLIDE of Megara*, London. Facsimile edn, Neale Watson Academic Publications, 1975.

DelaHaye, J.-P. (1989) 'Chaitin's equation: an extension of Gödel's theorem' *Notices of the American Mathematical Society* 36: 984–7.

Deleuze, G. (1984) *Kant's Critical Philosophy:The Doctrine of the Faculties*, trans. H. Tomlinson and B. Habberjam, Athlone Press, London, University of Minnesota Press, Minneapolis.

Derrida, J. (1977) 'Signature Event Context', trans. S. Weber and J. Mehlman, in his *Glyph I*, Johns Hopkins University Press, Baltimore.

Derrida, J. (1983) 'The time of a thesis: punctuations' in A. Montefiore (ed.) *Philosophy in France Today*, Cambridge University Press, Cambridge.

Descartes, R. (1925) *The Geometry of René Descartes* by D. E. Smith and M. L. Latham, Open Court, Chicago, IL, and London 1925. Translation of *La Géométrie* published as an appendix to *Discours de la Méthode*, 1637.

Descartes, R. (1931) 'Rules of the direction of the mind' in *The Philosophical Works of Descartes*, trans. and ed. E. S. Haldane and G. R. T. Ross, Cambridge University Press, Cambridge. 2nd edn, Dover, New York, 1955.

Donoghue, D. (1983) *The Arts Without Mystery*, British Broadcasting Corporation, London.

Dummett, M. (1963) 'The philosophical significance of Gödel's theorem', *Ratio* V, pp. 140–55; reprinted in Dummett (1978).

Dummett, M. (1967) 'Frege' entry in P Edwards (ed.) *Encyclopedia of Philosophy*, Macmillan, New York. Reprinted in Dummett (1978).

Dummett, M. (1978) *Truth and Other Enigmas*, Duckworth, London.

Eldridge, R. (1985) 'Deconstruction and its alternatives', *Man and World 18*, pp. 147–70.

Euclid (1926) *The Thirteen Books of Euclid's Elements*, trans. T. L. Heath, Cambridge University Press, Cambridge. 2nd ed., reprinted Dover, New York, 1956.

Field, H. (1980) *Science Without Numbers*, Blackwell, Oxford.

Frege, G. (1879) *Begriffsschrift, eine der arithmetischen nachgebildete Formelsprache des reinen Denkens*, Nebert, Halle. English trans. Frege (1972).

Frege, G. (1884) *Die Grundlagen der Arithmetik. Eine logisch-mathematische Untersuchung über den Begriff der Zahl*, Koebner, Breslau. English trans. Frege (1953).

Frege, G. (1893) *Grundgesetze der Arithmetik, begriffsschriftlich abgeleitet*, vol. 1, Pohle, Jena. Partial English trans. Frege (1964).

Frege, G. (1924–25) 'A new attempt at a foundation of arithmetic' in Frege (1979).

Frege, G. (1950) *The Foundations of Arithmetic*, trans. of Frege (1884) by J. L. Austin, Blackwell, Oxford.

Frege, G. (1964) *The Basic Laws of Arithmetic: Exposition of the System*, partial translation of Frege (1893) by M. Furth, University of California Press, Berkeley and Los Angeles, CA.

Frege, G. (1971) *On the Foundations of Geometry and Formal Theories of Arithmetic*, trans. and ed. E. H. Kluge, Yale University Press, London and New Haven, CT.

Frege, G. (1972) *Conceptual Notation and Related Articles*, trans. of Frege (1879) by T. W. Bynum, Clarendon Press, Oxford.

Frege, G. (1979) *Gottlob Frege: Posthumous Writings*, Blackwell, Oxford.

Friedman, H. (1976) 'Systems of second order arithmetic with restricted induction I, II' (abstracts) *Journal of Symbolic Logic* 41:557–9.

Gardies, J.-L. (1984) *Pascal entre Eudoxe et Cantor*, Libraire Philosophique, J. Vrin, Paris.

Gaukroger, S. (1989) *Cartesian Logic: An Essay on Descartes' Conception of Inference*, Clarendon Press, Oxford.

Gentzen, G. (1936) 'Die Widerspruchsfreiheit der reinen Zahlentheorie' *Mathematische Annalen*, 112:493–565. Translated as 'The Consistency of elementary number theory' in M. E. Szabo (ed.) (1969) *The Collected Papers of Gerhard Gentzen*, North-Holland, Amsterdam.

Gleick, J. (1987) *Chaos: Making a New Science*, Penguin Books, New York.

Gödel, K. (1930) 'The completeness of the axioms of the functional calculus of Logic' in van Heijenhoort (1967).

Gödel, K. (1931) 'On formally undecidable propositions of *Principia Mathematica* and related systems I' in van Heijenhoort (1967) and Davis (1965).

Gödel, K. (1944) 'Russell's mathematical logic' in P. A. Schilpp (ed.) *The Philosophy of Bertrand Russell*, The Library of Living Philosophers,

Taylor Publishing, Evanston, IL. Reprinted in Benacerraf and Putnam (1964) and (1983).

Hacking, I. (1973) 'Leibniz and Descartes' proof and eternal truths', *Proceedings of the British Academy*, LIX.

Harrington, L. A., Morley, M. D., Scedrov, A. and Simpson, S. G. (eds) (1985) *Harvey Freidman's Research on the Foundations of Mathematics*, North-Holland, Amsterdam.

Hilbert, D. (1899) *Grundlagen der Geometrie*, Teubner, Stuttgart. Trans. as *Foundations of Geometry*, Open Court, La Salle, IL, 1971.

Hilbert, D. (1900) 'The future of mathematics', Chapter X of Reid (1970).

Hilbert, D. (1904) 'On the foundations of logic and arithmetic' in van Heijenhoort (1967).

Hilbert, D. (1925) 'On the infinite' in van Heijenhoort (1967) and Benacerraf and Putnam (1964) and (1983).

Hilbert, D. (1927) 'The foundations of mathematics' in van Heijenhoort (1967).

Hilbert, D. (1971) 'The correspondence between Frege and Hilbert' in Frege (1971).

Hofstadter, D. R. (1979) *Gödel, Escher, Bach: an Eternal Golden Braid*, Basic Books, New York and Harvester Press, Hassocks, Sussex.

Hume, D. (1748) *An Enquiry Concerning Human Understanding*. Modern edition, *An Enquiry Concerning the Human Understanding and Concerning the Principles of Morals*, ed. L. A. Selby-Bigge, Oxford University Press, Oxford, 1902.

Kant, I. (1929) *Critique of Pure Reason*, trans. N. Kemp Smith, Macmillan, London. Originally published as *Kritik der reinen Vernunft*, Hartknoch, Riga, 1787.

Kant, I. (1951) *Critique of Judgement*, trans. J. H. Bernard, Hafner Press, Macmillan, New York.

Kitcher, P. (1983) *The Nature of Mathematical Knowledge*, Oxford University Press, New York.

Kline, M. (1980) *Mathematics: the Loss of Certainty*, Oxford University Press, Oxford.

Kneale, W. and Kneale, M. (1962) *The Development of Logic*, Clarendon Press, Oxford.

Lachterman, D. R. (1989) *The Ethics of Geometry: a Genealogy of Modernity*, Routledge, New York and London.

Locke, J. (1689) *Essay Concerning Human Understanding*, Churchill, London.

Löwenheim, L. (1915) 'On possibilities in the calculus of relatives' in van Heijenhoort (1967).

Maddy, P. (1984) 'New directions in the philosophy of mathematics', *Philosophy of Science Association 2*, pp. 427–48.

Manheim, J. H. (1964) *The Genesis of Point Set Topology*, Pergamon, Oxford, London, Paris, Frankfurt, and Macmillan, New York.

Nerlich, G. (1976) *The Shape of Space*, Cambridge University Press, Cambridge.

Paris, J. and Harrington, L. (1977) 'A mathematical incompleteness in

Peano arithmetic' in J. Barwise (ed.) *Handbook of Mathematical Logic*, North-Holland, Amsterdam.

Peano, G. (1889) 'The principles of arithmetic presented by a new method' in J. van Heijenoort (ed.) *From Frege to Gödel*, Harvard University Press, Cambridge, MA, 1967.

Poster, M. (1989) *Critical Theory and Poststructuralism: In Search of a Context*, Cornell University Press, Ithaca, NY, and London.

Prigogine, I and Stengers, I. (1984) *Order out of Chaos*, Bantam Books, Toronto and New York.

Putnam, H. (1975) 'What is mathematical truth?' in his *Mathematics, Matter and Method*, Cambridge University Press, Cambridge.

Quine, W. O. (1948) 'On what there is', *Review of Metaphysics*, reprinted in his *From a Logical Point of View*, Harvard University Press, Cambridge, MA., 1953.

Quine, W. O. (1960) *Word and Object*, MIT Press, Cambridge, MA.

Reid, C. (1970) *Hilbert*, Springer-Verlag, Berlin.

Resnik, M. D. (1980) *Frege and the Philosophy of Mathematics*, Cornell University Press, Ithaca, NY, and London.

Resnik, M. D. (1988) 'On the philosophical significance of consistency Proofs' in Shankar (1988a).

Russell, B. (1897) *Foundations of Geometry*, Cambridge University Press, Cambridge.

Russell, B. (1903) *Principles of Mathematics*, Cambridge University Press, Cambridge.

Russell, B. (1919) *Introduction to Mathematical Philosophy*, Allen & Unwin, London.

Russell, B. (1912) *The Problems of Philosophy*, The Home University Library, Allen & Unwin, London. Reprinted by Oxford University Press, 1959.

Scott, D. (1970) 'Semantic Archaeology: a parable', *Synthese* 21: 399–407.

Shankar, S. G. (ed.) (1988a) *Gödel's Theorem in Focus*, Croom Helm, London, New York, Sydney.

Shankar, S. G. (1988b) 'The dawning of (machine) intelligence', *Philosophica* 43 I.

Simpson, S. G. (1985) 'Big news from Archimedes to Freidman' in Harrington *et al.* (1985).

Simpson, S. G. (1987) 'Subsystems of Z_2 and reverse mathematics' in G. Takeuti *Proof Theory*, North-Holland, Amsterdam.

Simpson, S. G. (1988) 'Partial realizations of Hilbert's Program', *Journal of Symbolic Logic* 53(2), 349–63.

Skolem, T. (1920) 'Logico-combinatorial investigations in the satisfiability or provability of mathematical propositions: a simplified proof of a theorem by L. Löwenheim and generalizations of the theorem' in van Heijenhoort (1967).

Skolem, T. (1922) 'Some remarks on axiomatized set theory' in van Heijenhoort (1967).

Smorynski, C. (1985) 'The varieties of arboreal experience' and 'Some rapidly growing functions' in Harrington *et al.* (1985).

Smorynski, C. (1988) 'Hilbert's Program', University of Utrecht, Department of Mathematics, preprint UR522.

Smullyan, R. (1987) *Forever Undecided: A Puzzle Guide to Gödel*, Alfred A. Knopf, New York.

Stewart, I. (1987) *The Problems of Mathematics*, Oxford University Press, Oxford.

Stewart, I. (1989) *Does God Play Dice?*, Blackwell, Oxford.

Tarski, A. (1931) 'The concept of truth in formalized languages' in his *Logic, Semantics and Metamathematics*, trans. J. H. Woodger, Clarendon Press, Oxford, 1956.

Tiles, M. (1984) *Bachelard: Science and Objectivity*, Cambridge University Press, Cambridge.

Tiles, M. (1989) *Philosophy of Set Theory: an Historical Introduction to Cantor's Paradise*, Blackwell, Oxford.

Tragasser R. (1984) *Husserl: Mathematical Realism*, Cambridge University Press, Cambridge.

van Heijenhoort, J. (1967) *From Frege to Gödel*, Harvard University Press, Cambridge, MA.

van Fraasen, B. (1970) *An Introduction to the Philosophy of Time and Space*, Random House, New York.

von Neumann, J. (1931) 'Die formalistische Grundlegung der Mathematik' *Erkenntnis* 2. Translated as 'The formalist foundations of mathematics' in Benacerraf and Putnam (1983).

Wang, H. (1986) *Beyond Analytic Philosophy*, MIT Press, Cambridge, MA.

Weyl, H. (1970) 'David Hilbert and his mathematical work' in Reid (1970).

Whitehead, A. N. and Russell, B. (1910–13) *Principia Mathematica*, 3 vols, Cambridge University Press, Cambridge.

Wittgenstein, L. (1922) *Tractatus Logico-Philosophicus*, 1st edn. with English translation. Translation by D. F. Pears and B. F. McGuiness, Routledge and Kegan Paul, London, 1961.

Wittgenstein, L. (1956) *Remarks on the Foundations of Mathematics*, Blackwell, Oxford.

INDEX